"This Vast Pollution . . ."

"This Vast Pollution . . ."

United States of America
v.
Reserve Mining Company

by

Thomas F. Bastow

Green Fields Books
Washington, D.C.

1986

345.0242
B327

Design and Typography by Henry Taylor
Jacket Design by John Yanson
Manufactured in the United States of America
        by Arcata Graphics Company
Published by Green Fields Books
        Post Office Box 8228
        Washington, D.C., 20024
First Edition
Library of Congress Catalog Card Number: 86–80697
ISBN 0-937715-01-8

For Edward and Rosemary Bastow

CONTENTS

Foreword

Every writer brings a personal point of view to his subject. I grew up in Michigan on the shores of the Great Lakes. As soon as I had completed law school and a tour of duty in the Navy, I went to work for the litigation office of the newly-created U.S. Environmental Protection Agency in Washington. For the next four years I was a trial lawyer, first for EPA, and then for the Natural Resources Division of the U.S. Department of Justice. During those years, the Federal government's effort to stop the Reserve Mining Company from dumping its wastes into Lake Superior dominated my waking hours: I worked, ate, drank, and talked with the people who appear on the pages of this book.

I cannot claim that this is the book of a disinterested, impartial observer (if there is such a thing), but I have taken great pains to make it an accurate book. Aided by a generous grant from Resources for the Future, Inc., I spent a year searching hundreds of thousands of pages of government and personal files, and interviewing every person of importance in this controversy who would speak to me. The central figures in this book were each interviewed face-to-face at least twice. (All of the quotations in this book which are introduced in the present tense are the products of such interviews.)

When I have presented an event as an historical fact, I have relied upon the present recollection of an eyewitness whom I have found reliable, corroborated by an independent recollection or by contemporary documents. Where corroboration has not been possible I have identified my single source. Unfortunately, the men who conducted Reserve Mining Company's defense against the federal government refused to be interviewed. So I have relied, in presenting the internal actions of Reserve and its parent corporations, on subpoenaed corporate records and the sworn testimony of corporate officers on file with the U.S. District Court for the District of Minnesota.

In order to achieve a concise and comprehensible narrative, I have omitted from this book the names of many public servants who devoted themselves to stopping Reserve's dumping. My apologies to them. I hope that I will not compound my offense by making special mention of four fellow lawyers: Bradford F. Whitman, whose hard work for the Natural Resources Division of the Department of Justice was important to this and other landmark environmental cases, and three Minnesotans whose courageous work on this case was undertaken at no small risk to their professional careers — Byron E. Starns, the State's aggressive and talented Chief Deputy Attorney General, Philip L. Olfelt, a dedicated Assistant Attorney General, and Howard J. Vogel, whose representation of environmental groups was worth many times his fee.

Many people have helped me to write this book. My collaborator, Chris Bastow, worked both ends of the book-writing machine, cranking in background research and editing the output. The rest of my family and my friends have tolerated my obsession with good humor. Nancy Matthews, my able secretary when I was at EPA, has worked on her own time, typing this manuscript through many drafts. Pamela Quinn and John Varnum, the lawyers who succeeded me at EPA and the Department of Justice, put up with my constant demands on the government's files. When all other sources of information failed, I frequently had recourse to the cluttered, windowless office of H.R. Reinhardt, whose extensive personal knowledge was the closest thing EPA had to an institutional memory.

Finally, I could never have written this book without the steadfast advice and encouragement of another lawyer, John Michael Roach, through the years it took to live and write the story told here.

"This Vast Pollution . . ."

I

Unofficial Reports

On a bright August day in 1967, a career scientist for the Federal government named Donald Mount drove his six year-old Volkswagen along the western edge of Lake Superior into Duluth, Minnesota. Mount glanced from time to time at his wife, seated beside him, as she looked with disappointment at Duluth's decayed downtown and abandoned docks — evidence that this city of 100,000 had passed its heyday as the chief port for the shipment of high grade ore from the Mesabi Iron Range, just inland. Mount's job required that he make the best of the city. He had just been named the director of a new Federal laboratory and he was coming to Duluth for the dedication of the striking glass-and-brick laboratory building on the residential outskirts of town.

Mount's new job was a result of the Federal government's expanding role in combatting water pollution. A series of statutes, shaped in the Public Works Committees of the United States Congress over the last 10 years, authorized millions of dollars in federal grants to help cities clean up their sewage. The laws also directed the Federal government to cooperate with the States in making industrial dischargers meet acceptable water quality standards, and to increase its own research and development on water pollution. A new Federal Water Pollution Control Administration had been created in the United States Department of the Interior. This agency had built new laboratories to carry out the larger research program that the laws called for — and it had built them in the districts of influential Congressmen. A major water pollution research facility was built in Oklahoma, the home state of the Chairman of the Senate Public Works Committee. And the

1

National Water Quality Laboratory was built in the district of Minnesota's John A. Blatnik, a senior member of the House Public Works Committee and the sponsor of all the major pollution control legislation recently adopted by the Congress. Congressman Blatnik was proud of "his" laboratory, even if he viewed his role in sponsoring water pollution control laws as of secondary importance. (Looking back on his long legislative career, Blatnik identifies his most important accomplishments as those which brought jobs to his economically depressed district. A political ally who drafted most of Blatnik's pollution control bills says, "John Blatnik was essentially a builder and a public works man — he had no more than a general interest in enforcing pollution control.")

The new Federal Water Pollution Control Administration had selected Donald Mount, a bright young biologist from Ohio, over dozens of more senior scientists as the first director of the National Water Quality Laboratory (although Mount had been required to hire an old political supporter of Congressman Blatnik from the Duluth Water Department as his assistant before his appointment was approved). Mount had been in the forefront of the Federal government's fight against water pollution as an employee of the Division of Water Supply and Pollution Control of the United States Public Health Service, the predecessor of the new agency. Growing up on a small Ohio farm, Mount had been fascinated by animal life as long as he could remember. As a boy, he had kept mice, snakes, spiders, anything that moved, as pets. After he earned a Ph. D. in fish toxicology from Ohio State University, he found that the Public Health Service at Cincinnati was one of the few places where he could continue the research he loved. His reputation had spread beyond the laboratory as a result of his discovery of the cause of large, seemingly inexplicable, fish kills on the lower Mississippi River in the early 1960's. By November 1963, the fish kills had reached such proportions that State authorities had asked the Public Health Service for help. Mount had gone to the scene. He later reported:

> We saw dying fish in the river and canals in the Baton
> Rouge area and in the passes of the Mississippi River
> near the coastal town of Venice, Louisiana. Channel

catfish, drum, buffalo and shad were most affected, but we also observed acres of minnows at the surface that would convulse when stressed by our boat. In the brackish water area, mullet and menhaden were observed jumping several feet out of the water when disturbed by the wake of our boat; frequently we saw them land on the levees or oil well platforms.

Back in Cincinnati, with the aid of a technician, Mount conducted weeks of painstaking laboratory tests, ruling out botulism, viruses and toxic concentrations of metals, as causes of the fish kill. One day, he was about to throw out a lone guppy which had been living for weeks in a test bottle with distilled water and sterilized extracts of Mississippi River sediments. As he reached for the bottle, the guppy went into convulsions. Some chemical present in the river and its sediments was almost the only possible cause that Mount had not already eliminated. He conducted more weeks of testing and submitted samples for chemical analysis by newly-acquired gas chromatographs, finally identifying toxic levels of the chemical pesticide endrin in the river sediments. He was able to trace the cause of the fish kills back to discharges from a plant of the Velsicol Chemical Corporation engaged in manufacturing endrin on the Mississippi River at Memphis, Tennessee. Soon Mount was lecturing visiting laymen and Congressmen on his findings: he had a large channel catfish in a fifty-gallon tank on the stage behind him; at the beginning of his lecture, he added a drop of endrin to the tank — less than 20 parts of endrin for every billion parts of water; while he spoke, the fish behind him hemmorhaged, went into convulsions, leaped out of the tank, and lay thrashing on the floor. The lower Mississippi River fish kill, Mount recalls, was "a real detective job, the most fun I'd ever had," and it made his name as a scientist.

Although he was in his mid-thirties, his dark hair receding, the new director of the National Water Quality Laboratory still looked like the sort of bright earnest boy who helped you through your science lab — he was all arms and legs, he smiled shyly, and his head and Adam's apple bobbed nervously when he spoke. Mount sat down at his desk after the laboratory building had been dedicated and the dignitaries had departed. He admired his view

3

across the rolling lawn of the laboratory to Lake Superior, the largest expanse of fresh water in the world. The northernmost of the Great Lakes, Lake Superior was the least marred by pollution; from the mid-19th to the mid-20th century, water quality, while declining dramatically on the other lakes, had remained remarkably stable here. Mount looked at his desk. It did not have a piece of paper on it or in it. What, he wondered, happens next?

Mount had never heard of the Reserve Mining Company, a subsidiary of two of the nation's largest industrial corporations, Armco Steel and Republic Steel. He did not know that this company, operating at Silver Bay, Minnesota, just 50 miles up the shore of Lake Superior from his laboratory, was dumping more solid waste into the water every day than the next ten largest industrial polluters in the United States combined.

* * *

The Great Depression hit the miners on Minnesota's Mesabi Iron Range particularly hard. As demand shrank, tonnages of ore shipped from the Range fell by more than 50 percent. Also, because of mechanization, fewer men were needed to produce a ton of iron ore. And the available high-grade ore was fast being used up. Professor E. W. Davis of the University of Minnesota Mines Experiment Station had been working for 25 years on a potential source of thousands of new mining jobs — a method of turning taconite, a hard, low-grade iron ore abundant in northern Minnesota, into a superior feed material for steel blast furnaces. Davis recounts in his lucid memoir, *Pioneering with Taconite*, that he had the engineering problems of processing taconite fairly well in hand in 1940 when he gained an audience with the vice president for operations of Republic Steel — only to have the executive tell him Republic wouldn't be interested in "that God-damned hard stuff or anything else out there in Minnesota until you get over the idea of taxing everything to death." Davis saw that he would have to change the tax laws in order to realize his vision of economic improvement for his depressed region, so he

4

patiently turned his attention from engineering to politics. He had William K. Montague, a Duluth lawyer who represented the steel industry, draft a bill for the State Legislature effectively prohibiting all property taxes on taconite while it was still in the ground. Then Davis recruited a young legislator from the Range named John A. Blatnik, who got the bill enacted into law in 1941. Within three years, major steel companies were financing four separate pilot taconite projects in Minnesota.

One of these pilot projects was operated at the town of Babbitt, on the east Mesabi Range, by the Reserve Mining Company. The parent steel companies named their subsidiary "Reserve," because they were developing taconite as a resource that they might not need for twenty years. By 1947, however, Reserve Mining Company applied to the State for permission to begin the first full-scale production of iron from taconite. Ore would be mined at Babbitt and rail-hauled 47 miles to Silver Bay, Minnesota, for "beneficiation." During the beneficiation process, the taconite, suspended in a stream of water, would be crushed to the fineness of flour; iron would be magnetically separated and formed into pellets; the pellets would be loaded onto ore boats for shipment; and the waste rock (called tailings) would be dumped into Lake Superior. The completed project would employ 3,000 men. Before granting Reserve the permits necessary to begin operations, the State Departments of Conservation and Health held a series of public hearings over the course of five months. Reserve Mining Company's case for issuance of the permits, presented by William K. Montague, included the support of a broad range of northeastern Minnesota civic and conservation organizations. No one at the hearings opposed Reserve's plans to strip-mine, process, and ship taconite; and only two groups, both from Duluth, opposed the dumping of tailings into Lake Superior at Silver Bay. Professor Davis and Reserve's manager both testified that it would cost an additional 95 cents per ton of iron pellets produced (compared to a selling price of only $5.05 per ton) to pump water, buy the power to crush ore, and maintain a tailings impoundment at Babbitt, instead of going ahead with the project at Silver Bay as proposed. "We have to cut every cent off the cost that we can," they warned; the steel companies had to "convince themselves that [Minnesota] taconite is the cheapest source of iron ore available," otherwise, "it will be necessary to go out of the State of Minnesota to find that ore, and in the next five years that is what we will do."

Montague presented testimony that Reserve's tailings, consisting mainly of silica, would be inert in water. Two hydraulic engineers from the University of Minnesota testified about test tank experiments performed at the University for the company. On the basis of these experiments, they predicted that coarser tailings discharged from the plant at Silver Bay would settle out immediately, building up a beach or delta on the shore of Lake Superior. Finer tailings would form a density current and flow down the face of the delta to the bottom of the lake, 800 feet deep. Because there were no natural currents deep in the lake, the fine tailings would settle out there. Ordinarily, there would be no visible discoloration of the lake beyond "a couple of thousand feet." At worst, during storms, the lake might be clouded "on the order of a mile."

Duluth members of the United Northern Sportsmen Club (an affiliate of the National Wildlife Federation) and the Brotherhood of Railway Trainmen (an old-line AFL craft union), representing themselves, presented the case against Reserve. A railroad worker argued: "I feel this way, gentlemen, ladies, if there is any here . . . . I like to see industry but it is a poor industry that can't take care of its waste. It ain't worthwhile having." A member of United Northern Sportsmen supported him: "I would like to go along with Brother Tuskey . . . . If we remember back, we are all kicking ourselves for the steal that our timber barons made in this country . . . . As I see it, it is just another case with Lake Superior being robbed the same as northern Minnesota was robbed of its timber."

The United Northern Sportsmen presented commercial fishermen who concluded, on the basis of clinkers and debris caught in their nets, that there was a strong current, hundreds of feet deep in Lake Superior, running southwest past Silver Bay toward Duluth. An officer of the Brotherhood of Railway Trainmen introduced a letter from a man living on an inland lake polluted by mining wastes: "The silt from the tailings will never settle . . . . You can have a glass full from any Duluth faucet in about four years from now if this project goes through." A railroad worker warned, "That rock when it is crushed, . . . there will be . . . sharp points on it, approximately the same as ground glass will be, and any of you know that eating a little ground glass will put you about across the divide." Members of United Northern Sportsmen said the Duluth public health officer had warned them that the city would probably have to build a filtration plant to protect its water supply from contamination by tailings. They asked if Reserve would furnish a bond against harming the City's water supply. William Montague replied that the State had long ago requested Duluth to filter its water, and

> We are certainly not going to say that if the City of Duluth eventually puts in a filtration plant that we are to be the ones to pay for it under those circumstances. I assume that the City of Duluth has the same right which any other private person would have against the Reserve Mining Company of maintaining an action in the event they could prove damage.

One week before the final hearing on Reserve's permits, the Duluth public health officer backed down. In a letter to the City Council, he noted the absence of scientific evidence about currents deep in Lake Superior. He concluded:

> It is a well-known fact that the inhalation of silica dust is capable of producing a distinct disease known as silicosis, but there is no evidence to support the belief that the swallowing of silica is particularly harmful to the human system. This statement is not to be construed as an argument in support of the Mining Company's request for permission to run the tailings into Lake Superior, but is offered merely as one of the reasons why we find ourselves unable to offer a conclusive or irrefutable reason for its denial.

In December 1947, Minnesota granted Reserve a permit to discharge tailings into Lake Superior, subject to a number of conditions. For example, the discharge was not to include

7

material quantities of any substance soluble in water or to cause material clouding or discoloration or nuisance conditions outside a nine square-mile zone of the lake or to have any material adverse effect on public water supplies. Nearly twenty years later, Professor Davis wrote of the permit hearings: "It became obvious that the opposition was trying to . . . delay the construction of a taconite plant on the lake shore. Why they were doing this was never clear to me." A senior official of the State Department of Conservation was less mystified than Davis: "We looked into who was behind the opposition to Reserve," he said. "It was the Communists." Shortly after issuance of the State permits, the United States Army Corps of Engineers, which controlled navigation on the country's inland waters, also issued Reserve the only Federal permit it needed, to construct a breakwater and deposit tailings at Silver Bay.

The E. W. Davis Works of Reserve Mining Company began production at Silver Bay in October 1955. In 1964, the citizens of Minnesota provided a further incentive to development of the taconite industry; they adopted, by a 7-1 margin, an amendment to the State Constitution prohibiting for 25 years any increase in the rate of occupation, royalty, and use taxes paid by the taconite industry. The campaign for the Taconite Amendment was led by the Democratic-Farmer-Labor party (DFL); prominent members supporting the amendment included Senator Hubert H. Humphrey and Congressman John Blatnik. By this time Congressman Blatnik was a close personal friend and frequent guest of Reserve Mining Company's president; every operating officer of Reserve supported Blatnik with political contributions.

The taconite industry boomed after the adoption of the Taconite Amendment. American steel companies built half a dozen new full-sized beneficiation plants in Minnesota — all, however, located on the Mesabi Iron Range with closed-circuit recirculating water systems, and not on the shore of Lake Superior like the Reserve Mining Company plant. By 1967, Reserve had expanded its operation until it was shipping to Armco and Republic Steel 12% of all the iron mined in the United States. There was a by-product: every day from the Reserve plant 67,000 tons of tailings in 700 million gallons of water crashed from two chutes in opaque gray waterfalls 15 feet wide and 10 feet high, merging to form a river 4 to 6 inches deep and a quarter-mile wide, which flowed across a delta of coarse tailings into Lake Superior.

.   .   .

The new director of the National Water Quality Laboratory and most other citizens of Minnesota were unaware of any damage that Reserve Mining Company might be causing to Lake Superior. However, Reserve's discharge into the lake was beginning to awaken concern. Since 1956 — Reserve's first full year of operation — commercial fishermen along the Minnesota shore of Lake Superior had been complaining about stretches miles long, where the clear blue water of the lake was changed to a cloudy green; about gray slimes growing on their nets; and about reduced fish catches. In response to these complaints, water pollution scientists working for the Minnesota Department of Health conducted an investigation in the fall of 1956 and again in the summer of 1957. They reported that cloudy "green water" could be seen frequently near Silver Bay in 1956 and even more frequently in 1957, when it extended from 3 miles northeast of the plant more than 35 miles down the shore to the southwest. There was much more suspended solid material in samples of this water than there was in samples of clear blue surface water taken from the lake near the Canadian border. When this material was filtered out, it "strongly resembled the natural gray-green color of taconite."

The samples were assigned code numbers and given to John Gruner, a professor of geology at the University of Minnesota, for analysis by x-ray diffraction. A glass prism, rotated in a beam of light, reflects rays of varying intensity. Similarly, mineral crystals, rotated in a beam of x-rays, reflect rays of varying intensity. An x-ray diffractometer records the angles at which a mineral sample reflects the most intense x-rays in a line-graph, or "pattern." Characteristic peaks in x-ray diffraction patterns may be used to identify the minerals in samples. Professor Gruner identified a major constituent of the solid material in the "green water" samples as a mineral of the amphibole group called cummingtonite-grunerite. The same mineral was a major constituent in samples of taconite tailings. (This mineral is found embedded in rock in the shape of small needles or fibers at various places around the world — its name derives from the town of Cummington, Massachusetts, and from a 19th century German geologist, E.F. Gruner. It was created in northern Minnesota by the intrusion of a mass of volcanic lava, called the Duluth Gabbro, at the eastern tip of the Mesabi Iron Range some 1,130 million years ago.) Professor Gruner reported that cummingtonite-grunerite was absent in the control samples taken near the Canadian border. It was also absent in a sample of lake sediment taken at Silver Bay before Reserve began operations. Professor Gruner concluded, "In all samples in which amphibole (grunerite-cummingtonite) is observed there can be no doubt that the mineral came from the east Mesabi Range."

The Minnesota Department of Health scientists also observed gray slimes on the nets of Lake Superior fishermen. They noted that much greater amounts of slime material were found on nets left in the lake for 1 day near Silver Bay than were found on nets left in the lake for 10 days near the Canadian border. These slimes were analyzed by microscope and by x-ray diffraction. The major constituents of the slimes found near Silver Bay were algae, iron-fixing bacteria and taconite tailings. The scientists ran a laboratory test. Pieces of nylon line similar to fish netting were suspended in beakers of Lake Superior water, and varying concentrations of taconite tailings were added to the beakers. More slime appeared to grow on the line as the concentrations of tailings were increased. This observation was confirmed by microscopic counts of algae and bacteria on the pieces of nylon line. The experiment was repeated with the same results.

The report of the 1956–1957 investigations by the water pollution scientists of the Minnnesota Department of Health was not made public for more than 10 years, however. Despite the existence of the report, Reserve Mining Company continued to maintain publicly that cummingtonite-grunerite was not a reliable tracer of its tailings, and the Department of Health (and the Minnesota Department of Conservation) continued to concede publicly that there was no evidence of pollution from Reserve's discharge. As one of the water pollution scientists later explained, "It was the philosophy of the Department at that time not to push."

By 1966, complaints about Reserve Mining Company's discharge reached beyond the State government. In that year, the first Federal scientists were transferred from Cincinnati to the temporary quarters of the National Water Quality Laboratory scattered around Duluth. One of these scientists, Dr. Louis Williams, was unhappy with the transfer. A Southerner, Williams did not want to struggle with Minnesota's bone-chilling winters, so he left his family in Cincinnati while he tried to get a warmer assignment. Williams had more than 20 years experience in aquatic biology, principally working with eutrophication, the process by which bodies of fresh water (like Lake Erie) become saturated with plant nutrients and grow old. Williams asserts in a soft, mournful drawl (and colleagues agree) that he had been treated shabbily in Cincinnati, despite his expertise. Now, in Duluth, with no laboratory director on the scene, there did not seem to be anything at all for him to do. Alone and at loose ends, Williams began talking to local fishermen and investigating the effects of Reserve Mining Company's discharge on Lake Superior.

Williams drove along the Minnesota shore taking samples from Lake Superior and its tributaries. He had samples taken for him, from the intake of Duluth's water supply, and by commercial fishermen in the open waters of the lake as far away as Wisconsin's Apostle Islands. He filtered the solids out of his samples and examined them by microscope at a magnification of 1000 times. In each sample from the lake, he counted algae and he found fine gray inorganic dust which he identified as taconite tailings. He sent samples to Cincinnati for chemical analysis by mass spectroscopy. Working in a converted men's room at the temporary quarters of the laboratory, he added varying concentrations of tailings to samples of lake water in order to study the effect on naturally-occurring algae populations.

Williams found no support from his supervisors for his investigation of Reserve Mining Company's discharge. In fact, he recalls that shortly after he addressed a civic group on the subject of Reserve, the acting director of the laboratory visited Duluth and warned him to stay away from "sensitive" research areas. His speech had come to the attention of Federal Water Pollution Control Administration headquarters in Washington. Dr. Leon Weinberger, the agency's assistant commissioner for research and development later explained: "He had no clearance. It's upsetting to have someone give information like this to an after-dinner group when you haven't checked it out to see that it's accurate."

Unable either to find another job with the agency or to win assurances he would have a meaningful job in Duluth, Williams resigned from the Federal service for a university professorship in August 1967, just before discovering that his old friend and colleague from Cincinnati, Don Mount, was the new director of the National Water Quality Laboratory. On Mount's arrival in Duluth, Williams told him he was sorry he had quit; he was sure they could have worked together. Mount wasn't so sure — Williams' manner of speaking and writing approached free association. Questioning him on a scientific subject was like panning for gold: one had to have a quick eye for a few shining nuggets in a large volume of extraneous pebbles. While Mount respected Williams' competence as a laboratory worker, he thought Williams had no feel for the scientific analysis of data.

Before he left Duluth, Williams took steps to see that the results of his work on Reserve would not simply disappear into the government's files, as had the earlier work done for the State. He wrote to Gaylord Nelson, a liberal Democratic U.S. Senator from Wisconsin with a strong environmental record, saying that his work had substantiated charges that Reserve Mining Company was polluting Lake Superior. Williams also wrote to Martin Hanson, the secretary of the Wisconsin Resource Conservation Council, a citizen organization that Nelson had established when he was governor of Wisconsin. Hanson released Williams' letter to the press in September 1967. The letter did not mention Reserve Mining Company by name, but it said that Williams' "preliminary studies seem to indicate that we have a basis now to be gravely concerned about the deterioration of the water quality of Lake Superior." Specifically, Williams' letter stated that distinctive gray taconite silt could be found on the bottom of Lake Superior from ten miles north of Silver Bay to Duluth, and to Wisconsin's Apostle Islands; that green water associated with taconite tailings was caused by colloidal particles refracting light, or by dense algae blooms, or both; that the absence of trace metals had apparently been a factor restricting the growth of algae in Lake Superior until now (here he noted that there had recently been a bloom of foul-smelling blue-green algae at the Duluth water intake); and finally that the effect of silting on important food chain organisms and on breeding grounds for fish should be investigated.

Williams' letter created a small political uproar. The Attorney General of Wisconsin used it to decry Reserve's pollution of Lake Superior in the press. The head of the Wisconsin Department of Natural Resources wrote to Donald Mount, asking how the National Water Quality Laboratory planned to follow up on Williams' research. Mount was not about to stake the scientific reputation of his new laboratory on Williams' statements; he wrote back that those statements appeared to be the "irresponsible results of 'bankside' observations . . . embellished with generous speculations." Twice, Mount wrote to Williams saying that he could not accept Williams' conclusions as a scientist, until he had seen his supporting data. He noted that Williams' letter contained only three hard pieces of data: an incubation temperature for algae growth, a single count of algae cells, and the depth of the Duluth water intake, 65 feet below the surface of Lake Superior. Williams responded, "I'll stand behind my preliminary conclusions." But he did not provide any data. Williams now says that his data books were stolen. Scientists who were at Duluth in 1967 can not recall his making such a claim at the time. Mount felt that he had been justified in dismissing Williams' work as mere "bankside observations." But, sometime after his exchange with Mount, Williams did publish two pieces of data — on concentrations of trace metals in green water and on concentrations of taconite tailings in western Lake Superior —

and these data have been confirmed by subsequent exhaustive investigations.

At the same time that he was dealing with the effects of Williams' letter, Mount received directions to supply office space at the laboratory to a man named Charles Stoddard, who was to fill the job of Regional Coordinator of the Interior Department's activities for the Upper Mississippi and Western Great Lakes. A quiet, solidly-built man with pale blue eyes and close-cut hair, Stoddard still had the command presence of a naval officer, twenty years after his service in World War II. Stoddard had been a conservationist since childhood, when he had gone with his father to meetings of the Izaak Walton League. A Federal scientist who worked with Stoddard says, "He's a real 'blue sky-er' — he believes in zero discharge as an industrial standard." Stoddard had worked for the U.S. Forest Service in the 30's and 40's. After seeing that many of the policy questions on which he had worked were finally decided by political pressures, Stoddard left the Federal government and became active in Democratic politics in his native northern Wisconsin. In the 1960 Presidential campaign, he worked first for Hubert Humphrey, then for John F. Kennedy. He was a high-level assistant to Kennedy's Secretary of the Interior, Stewart Udall, in Washington through the 60's. When Stoddard ran afoul of powerful timber interests early in 1967, he and Udall "agreed my usefulness was at an end." Tired of Washington, Stoddard secured the Regional Coordinator's job, which would take him close to home.

In the summer of 1967, before he moved into his Duluth office, Stoddard had taken a boat ride with his friends, Gaylord Nelson and Martin Hanson. Senator Nelson told Stoddard about his letter from Louis Williams. At Nelson's suggestion, Stoddard went to lunch with Williams in Duluth and heard his story. Thus, when Stoddard assumed his new duties, he was aware of the Reserve problem, but did not see any way that he could take action.

However, in the fall of 1967, Reserve Mining Company applied to the U.S. Army Corps of Engineers for an extension of its permit to deposit taconite tailings in Lake Superior. Pressed by the courts, the Corps was awakening to the fact that the projects which it permitted affected more than navigation. The Corps had just entered into an agreement with the Department of the Interior, under which the Corps' District Engineer was to notify the Department of any permit application and await the Department's advice as to how issuance of a permit might affect the environment. On November 1, 1967, the Minnesota district of the Corps of Engineers issued notice that Reserve Mining Company had applied for an extension of its permit, and the Regional Director of the Interior Department's Bureau of Sport Fisheries and Wildlife objected to the extension. Under newly issued regulations, it was Charles Stoddard's job to coordinate the responses of the Interior Department's numerous bureaus and agencies to the Corps of Engineers and to advise the Secretary of the Interior of any potential differences with the Corps. Now he had an opportunity to act.

With Secretary Udall's approval, Stoddard called a meeting of regional personnel from six Interior bureaus and agencies in February 1968. He also invited representatives of the Minnesota Pollution Control Agency (which had been created out of the old State Department of Health), the Minnesota Department of Conservation, and the Wisconsin Department of Natural Resources. To this group Stoddard proposed "a study of the problems associated with the disposal of taconite tailings into Lake Superior at Silver Bay." From the outset, Stoddard says, "I had the instinctive feeling it was dirt and it couldn't be good for Lake Superior. But I tried to be objective. I had no scientific reason to believe we'd find evidence of adverse effects. I just told them to call it straight and I'd take the heat." Donald Mount and other members of the Taconite Study Group were in no doubt, however, that Stoddard personally believed the protection of Lake Superior required Reserve to dump its tailings on land. Mount did not share Stoddard's belief. To be sure, his initial feeling had been that any industrial discharge as big as Reserve's "couldn't help but have a very bad effect on the lake." But he subsequently performed his own "crude and preliminary" toxicity test, putting fully-grown rainbow trout in undiluted tailings effluent. To his surprise, the fish "seemed happy for several weeks." The results were a vivid contrast with his work on the Velsicol Chemical

Corporation, Mount recalled, "and I began to wonder if there were any effects at all."

Stoddard's Taconite Study Group met again in March 1968 and adopted a work plan. Stoddard had no budgetary authority, but each regional director in the group agreed to scrounge the money necessary to carry out the plan from his regular budget. The Minneapolis office of the U.S. Bureau of Mines would analyze the feasibility of on-land tailings disposal. The St. Paul office of the U.S. Geological Survey would compare Reserve's discharge into Lake Superior with the sedimentation rates of natural tributaries. The Ann Arbor laboratory of the Bureau of Commercial Fisheries would examine fish catch statistics. The Lacrosse, Wisconsin, laboratory of the Bureau of Sport Fisheries and Wildlife would conduct a series of tests on the toxicity of tailings. The regional office of the Federal Water Pollution Control Administration in Chicago, assisted by the National Water Quality Laboratory, would conduct in-lake studies.

Scientists from the Duluth laboratory volunteered to investigate Reserve's discharge first-hand by a series of scuba dives. The divers observed that the tailings were indeed carried toward the bottom of Lake Superior by a density current, as Reserve had claimed in 1947. In fact, three experienced divers were caught in the plunging current one afternoon, and barely managed to struggle against it onto the tailings delta, where they sprawled exhausted, one of them unconscious. But the scuba divers also observed that the density current did not carry all of the tailings to the bottom. Each day they dove, they followed the density current as far as safety permitted, down about 100 feet, and each day they observed gray clouds billowing off the current. As the clouds gradually diffused down shore, they became a "green fog"; underwater visibility was commonly 5 feet in this green water, compared to visibility of 35 to 40 feet in clear water. The report of the scuba divers convinced Stoddard for the first time that the Taconite Study Group could come up with solid evidence of pollution.

The Taconite Study Group held five meetings during 1968. At these meetings, Stoddard would call on Interior Department personnel to give periodic progress reports and outline tentative conclusions on the blackboard. He was, Mount says, an effective manager. Stoddard set one meeting aside for the group to tour Reserve's operation and hear from representatives of United Northern Sportsmen and commercial fishermen, as well as from the company. "Bill Montague hounded us all the way through the committee's work," recalls Stoddard. Of Reserve's presentation, he says: "It just didn't square with the evidence we were gathering. It was bullshit."

Stoddard visited Washington in October and told Secretary Udall that his group appeared to have evidence of serious pollution. Udall cautioned him that he'd better take this up with Congressman Blatnik. After the October 25 meeting of the Taconite Study Group, the bureaus and agencies began writing their separate reports, and Donald Mount (with the help of an administrative staff man) began writing the conclusions for Stoddard's summary report to the Corps of Engineers. Mount still did not believe that the protection of Lake Superior necessarily required Reserve to dump its tailings on land, but, he says, "We tried to write conclusions which would support what we presumed would be Stoddard's recommendations, but which we could live with scientifically. I didn't know what Stoddard's power base was, but I knew he reported directly to Udall and I didn't want to antagonize the Department unnecessarily." Mount's conclusions included the following points:

(1) Reserve Mining Company discharged more sediments into Lake Superior in 12 days than all the lake's U.S. tributaries discharged into it in an entire year.

(2) Cummingtonite-grunerite was a reliable tracer of tailings in the lake.

(3) There was a counter-clockwise current in Lake Superior, running southwest past the plant, strong enough to carry fine tailings across State lines.

(4) Suspended tailings caused turbid, green water at least 18 miles southwest of the plant. (Mount noted in a separate report that spectrographic studies of green water samples had shown the color to be a result of the scattering of light by suspended tailings.)

(5) Widely accepted water quality criteria for lead, copper, zinc, cadmium, iron, and phosphorus were exceeded in the area of the discharge. (In the body of the report, some distance from the conclusions, Mount conceded that some of these elements were "presently insoluble, or at least biologically inactive.")

(6) Populations of bottom-dwelling organisms, especially one species important as a fish food, were reduced at least 15 miles southwest of the plant.

(7) Tailings effluent diluted with water by as much as 10 to one was lethal to infant rainbow trout in laboratory tests. However, even moderate changes in fish catches due to Reserve would have been masked by much larger changes in the fish population of Lake Superior due to the spread of predatory lamprey eels and overly-intensive commercial fishing.

(8) Reserve could afford to dispose of its tailings on land. (The Bureau of Mines suggested that Reserve could impound its tailings at a small inland lake called Lax Lake a few miles from Silver Bay, at an additional cost of roughly 40 cents per ton of iron pellets produced — compared to the current selling price of $12.80 per ton.)

Stoddard was pleased when he read Mount's conclusions, and he adopted them without change. He wrote out his recommendation as the Interior Department's Regional Coordinator that Reserve Mining Company be permitted to continue depositing tailings in Lake Superior only on the condition that Reserve construct on-land tailings disposal facilities and recycle its waste water, within three years. Neither Stoddard nor his study group gave explicit consideration to the environmental impact of dumping tailings on land rather than in the lake. So far as Stoddard was concerned, "the trade-off was simply between cleansing a big lake and sacrificing a small piece of land."

On November 5, 1968, while Stoddard's report was being drafted, Richard Nixon defeated Vice President Humphrey for the presidency after waging the most expensive campaign in American political history. Stoddard knew that as a political appointee he would be expected to resign once the new President was inaugurated. He feared that the Federal government's pursuit of Reserve Mining Company would end then. Reserve's board of directors was composed of officers of its parent corporations, Armco Steel and Republic Steel. According to a senior Republican Party official, Armco Steel's chief executive officer was a "heavy" in Republican politics in the days before campaign finance reform, with an influence comparable to the legendary Benjamin Fairless of U.S. Steel. So many officers of Republic Steel were prominent Nixon supporters, that Republic's regular board meeting was switched to Washington so that members could attend Nixon's inauguration on January 20, 1969.

At the beginning of December, Stoddard circulated Mount's draft summary report to the participants in the Taconite Study Group. The regional directors of the Interior bureaus and agencies all approved the draft. Stoddard felt that this was a sufficient consensus to put his draft in final form, although representatives of the State of Minnesota continued to side with Reserve. Stoddard and Mount, accompanied by Mount's assistant, then briefed Congressman Blatnik on the draft report at the Hotel Duluth. Blatnik was angry. "He did all the talking," Stoddard recalls. Blatnik didn't want the government "jumping to any conclusions" on the basis of one year's work: further research should be done. A week later, Stoddard recalls, he gave Secretary Udall a copy of his report and told him of Blatnik's reaction; the Secretary's only question to Stoddard was whether his report was scientifically honest. On December 31, 1968, following the Department's regulations, Regional Coordinator Stoddard submitted his final report and seven supporting studies to the Corps' District Engineer. He sent copies to Reserve Mining Company and to Max Edwards, the Assistant Secretary of the Interior for Water Quality, whose office was to prepare a news release in Washington.

Edwards, a young lawyer who had previously handled Congressional liaison for the Department, called Stoddard and suggested that he come to Washington: Congressman Blatnik was very disturbed about his report. In Washington Stoddard had lunch with Blatnik, who again suggested that the report should not be released, that more work should be done. Edwards' staff was still preparing a news release, but Stoddard was increasingly concerned that his report would be suppressed. Stoddard told

Senator Gaylord Nelson what was happening and urged him to lean on Secretary Udall to take the strongest action available to him under the Federal Water Pollution Control Act — calling a Federal-State enforcement conference on the interstate pollution of Lake Superior.

Back in Duluth, Stoddard confronted a stack of telephone messages from a cub reporter for the *Minneapolis Tribune* , Ron Way. Way wanted to know when the report of the Taconite Study Group would be out. After much hesitation, Stoddard told Way he could read the report if he came to Duluth. Way drove as fast as he could over icy roads to Duluth, hastily read and re-read the report, then wrote a story. He was so nervous about his scoop that before he drove back to Minneapolis, he put the story in an envelope and wrote on the envelope that it was to be given to his city editor in the event of accident. On Thursday, January 16, 1969, the lead story on the front page of the *Minneapolis Tribune* carried the headline: "U.S. STUDY FINDS TACONITE TAILINGS POLLUTE SUPERIOR." Stoddard had a number of copies of his report delivered to his office, and began sending them out in response to the numerous inquiries from people who had seen Way's story.

The out-going Administration in Washington reacted promptly to Stoddard's release of his report. Assistant Secretary Edwards said that the report was "unofficial"; it had to be reviewed in Washington; it contained "errors in conclusion" which Edwards would not specify. (Edwards' successor in the Nixon Administration was quick to endorse his position on Stoddard's report, labelling it "unofficial" and "unauthorized.") Congressman Blatnik hotly denied a *New York Times* story that the report was being suppressed through political influence. A Congressional colleague of Blatnik obtained a letter from Secretary Udall calling Stoddard's work merely "a preliminary staff report to develop the Department's official position." Udall wrote, "I can state to you categorically, that neither Representative Blatnik nor any other member of Congress intervened or attempted . . . to 'supress' any part of the Department's report on Lake Superior." Five years later Udall admitted to a reporter, "I don't come out with too much glory on this whole thing." Blatnik was "very upset" about

Stoddard's report, Udall said. "We needed his cooperation on a lot of things . . . and we sort of muffled our oars a little bit as a result of his remonstrations. Everyone agreed to kind of fudge it by saying it wasn't an official report. But it was all doubletalk. It *was* an Interior Department report. Blatnik and his people, in their effort to blunt it, were playing a lot of little games."

Even though Udall had "agreed to fudge it," Stoddard's report was before the public on the morning of January 16, 1969. Later that same day — the next-to-last working day of the out-going Administration — Secretary Udall called a Federal-State enforcement conference on the interstate pollution of Lake Superior. Senator Nelson had talked to Udall. Nelson had predicted that, if Udall did not call an enforcement conference, the Republican governor of Wisconsin would ask for one, and the new Administration would take all the political credit. (This prediction had been something of a bluff, since Nelson had no idea of the governor's intentions.) Udall says of the meeting, "Gaylord wasn't at all hesitant about pushing in his stack of chips." But, in assessing his reasons for calling the conference, Udall says "it really comes down to the work of one man — Chuck Stoddard."

On January 20, 1969, Donald Mount received a telephone call from the Department of the Interior in Washington. He was instructed to change the lock on Stoddard's office and see that no one entered.

II

Private Meetings, Public Protests

The conservation of publicly-owned natural resources has been a part of the program of American liberalism for most of the 20th century. On January 20, 1969, Richard Nixon brought to the Presidency very little record by which he could be judged on conservation issues, but he had been the bug-bear of American liberals for all of his twenty years in national politics. And he had not helped himself with conservationists by naming as his new Secretary of the Interior Walter J. Hickel. Hickel was a building contractor, an occupation often at swords' points with conservationists, and a successful Republican politican in Alaska, a state whose voters are enthusiastic for the exploitation of natural resources. Hickel had blundered at his first press conference after being named Secretary, by casually remarking that: "I think we have had a policy of conservation for conservation's sake." The outcry from conservationists had been loud and long.

Conservationists were not reassured when the most important Presidential appointments under Hickel at the Department of the Interior were made. The Department's new number two man was the least political and the best received. Under-Secretary Russell Train had been recommended to Hickel by Presidential Counsellor Peter Flanigan. Train had been a Republican appointee on the U.S. Tax Court in 1956, when he went on a safari and became interested in preserving African wildlife. At the time of his appointment, he was serving as president of the Conservation Foundation. Hickel's Assistant Secretary for Water Quality was Carl L. Klein, a heavy-set, cigar-smoking Republican ward committeeman and state legislator from suburban Chicago, an ally of conservative U.S. Senator Everett McKinley Dirksen. Klein had none of Senator Dirksen's mellifluous charm. Although he had long been interested in pollution control, even his supporters at the Department of the Interior regarded Klein as "a bull in a china shop." The new Commissioner of the Federal Water Pollution Control Administration was David D. Dominick, a young lawyer from Wyoming who had worked for his state's conservative U.S. Senator, Clifford Hansen, on the Senate Interior Committee. Dominick was also the nephew of another conservative U.S. Senator, Peter Dominick of Colorado. A *New York Times* editorial called the new team at the Department of the Interior "undistinguished as a group . . . political rather than professional," labelling Dominick's appointment "particularly disturbing."

Reserve Mining Company was one of the first problems confronted by Hickel's new team — "a ticking bomb," David Dominick called it. They quickly decided to request that the Army Corps of Engineers take no action on Reserve's application to extend its discharge permit, until the Lake Superior Enforcement Conference had made its recommendations. Under-Secretary Train formally made this request to the Chief of Engineers in March, effectively countermanding Charles Stoddard's request that the Corps require Reserve to construct a recirculating water system and quit dumping tailings into Lake Superior. This request allowed the Corps to forget about Reserve for the duration of the forthcoming enforcement conference — and enforcement conferences sometimes dragged on for years. Next, the team faced the problem of conducting the enforcement conference itself. Officers of Armco and Republic Steel were also considering this problem. They met at Cleveland in April 1969 to discuss methods of contacting government officials. That month, the executive vice presidents of Armco and Republic and the president of Reserve Mining Company met privately with Assistant Secretary Klein to discuss Reserve's pollution problem.

The Lake Superior Enforcement Conference would be held under the provisions of Congressman John Blatnik's Federal Water Pollution Control Act of 1961. The Act provided that enforcement conferences were to meet at the call of the Secretary of the Interior in cases where there was water pollution in one State that endangered the health or welfare of persons in another State. The pollution control agency of each interested State was to appoint representatives to the conference and the chairman of the conference was to give any alleged polluter an opportunity to make a full statement. The conferees were to draw conclusions as to the existence of interstate pollution and make recommendations for cleaning up the pollution. The Secretary of the Interior was then to prepare and forward a summary of these conclusions and recommendations to the conferees. The Act contained provisions that the Secretary could take further administrative actions leading to a request that the Department of Justice file suit against polluters who did not comply with conference recommendations. But these statutory provisions were so complicated and time-consuming that there had been only one such suit in the history of the Act. The main tool of an enforcement conference was not legal compulsion but public pressure.

The past master of conducting enforcement conferences and building public pressure was a career Federal lawyer, Murray Stein. In fact, David Dominick recalls, Stein was "the only master." A squat, blunt-spoken Brooklyn native, Stein had chaired nearly four dozen enforcement conferences during 20 years, first with the Public Health Service, then with the Federal Water Pollution Control Administration. In the early days Stein would investigate polluted streams himself. Then, armed with large supplies of cheap cigars and half-pint whiskey bottles, he would obtain affidavits establishing harm from hunters and "river rats." As interest in pollution control increased and more formal procedures were written into law, Stein began using dozens of speaking engagements and countless informal sessions with reporters to publicize cases of pollution identified by government river basin surveys. At public enforcement conference hearings held in hotel ballrooms, he cajoled representatives of States and industries, building a consensus on clean-up schedules. Then he returned for more public hearings on progress toward fulfilling those schedules. Stein was the logical man to chair the Lake Superior Enforcement Conference, but the new team at Interior felt they could not rely on his undivided loyalty; he was a

Democrat and a close ally of Congressman Blatnik. They decided that Assistant Secretary Klein and Commissioner Dominick would go with Stein to Duluth for the first session of the conference on May 13, 1969.

When Klein, Dominick and Stein arrived in Duluth, they found that they would not have needed to awaken public concern for the pollution of Lake Superior, even if they had wanted to. That public concern already existed in Duluth, even though the first Earth Day, April 22, 1970, was almost a year away. This nation-wide media event (a project of Senator Gaylord Nelson) is often cited as the beginning of widespread citizen action to protect the environment: at the time the Lake Superior Enforcement Conference opened, only 1% of the American population viewed pollution as an important problem; two years later, 25% of the population held this view.

Several factors have been advanced as causes of the citizens' environmental movement in the early 70's. First of all, visible pollution was increasing almost everywhere. In Ohio, for example, the Cuyahoga River actually caught fire at Cleveland, just four years after Murray Stein had first visited that city to open a Federal-State enforcement conference on the pollution of Lake Erie and its tributaries. Furthermore, the national economy was supporting a growing scientific community capable of documenting pollution which was not visible to the naked eye. In Texas, scientists provided detailed measurements of contamination in the rich shellfish beds of Galveston Bay from the grossly-polluted Houston Ship Channel nearby. At the end of the 50's, President Eisenhower had said that "water pollution is a uniquely local blight." By the end of the 60's, however, the media were making local environmental stories national news and citizens were aware of pollution as a widespread problem. The *Chicago Tribune* called the Cuyahoga River "a fire hazard." The "Houston Ship Channel" and "Galveston Bay" entries in the *New York Times Index* for a single year refer the reader to separate articles under "Water Pollution–Metals," "Water Pollution–Oil," and "Water Pollution–Sewage and Industrial Wastes." Citizen response to the government's role in environmental problems was also affected by the general political malaise. An increasingly educated public was no longer inclined to leave the solution of national problems to politicians: that public had recently witnessed the murders of three of America's most admired political leaders; far off in southeast Asia, the nation had gotten into the longest war in its history without any forthright explanation by the government; and many thoughtful people deeply distrusted the new President, Richard Nixon.

All of these factors helped to stir citizen action against pollution by 1971. These factors were also working on public opinion around the western end of Lake Superior in 1969. But something else was at work there that produced a grass-roots environmental movement years ahead of most of the country. That something else was a handful of exceptionally dedicated and able citizen leaders.

Grant Merritt, a 33 year-old lawyer and newly-elected town chairman of the Democratic–Farmer–Labor Party in suburban Minneapolis, received a visit from his uncle-by-marriage, Milton Mattson, in November 1967. For more than 50 years, Mattson's family had been commercial fishermen in Beaver Bay, Minnesota, a village just 3 miles down the shore of Lake Superior from Reserve Mining Company. Mattson gave Merritt a first-hand account of the slag Reserve was dumping into Lake Superior, the dirty green water, slime on fishing nets, and reduced catches. He told Merritt that Reserve's public relations office was dismissing green water as "an illusion." He also told him how Secretary of the Interior Udall had been scheduled to fly up the lake shore over the Reserve plant when he had dedicated the National Water Quality Laboratory that August and how Reserve had attempted to "fool" Udall by seeding its tailings delta with grass to pretty it up, just before his scheduled visit. As Merritt heard his uncle out, he became concerned that Reserve was ruining Lake Superior, and suspicious that Reserve was pulling the wool over the government's eyes. Since he had just entered politics, his first thought was that this was a political issue that could be developed and resolved through politics.

Grant Merritt's concern for Lake Superior was not impersonal. He had grown up in Duluth and played on the lake shore. From his childhood he had vacationed every summer at his family's cottage on Isle Royale in Lake Superior. He fondly recalls that as a boy he would stand on the bow of the slow boat to Isle Royale watching schools of herring deep in the clear water.

Merritt's family history also left him with what he calls "an inclination to be suspicious of the steel companies." Paul de Kruif recounts in his spellbinding popular history, *Seven Iron Men*, how Grant Merritt's grandfather, Alfred, and his brothers spent 20 years bushwhacking through the trackless forests of northern Minnesota, prospecting for iron. During a short-lived gold rush in 1865, Alfred Merritt's pioneer father picked up a few pieces of low-grade iron ore near the eastern end of the Mesabi Hills; at home in Duluth he told his sons, "There's iron up there worth more than all the gold in California." Working in the woods as surveyors and timber cruisers, the Merritt boys kept searching for iron, ignoring the opinions of mining companies and professional geologists. Alfred's brother, Leonidas, testified before a Congressional committee, "It was a matter of conscience with me . . . . I believed it was there because my father was a very intelligent man, and a man that did not go off the handle, and he had studied that up, and I believed it because he told me so, first."

In 1890 the Merritt brothers discovered the richest body of iron ore in America, the Mesabi Range. A boom was on. They borrowed heavily to open mines and connect them to Duluth with a new railroad. And within three years they lost everything to their creditors, John D. Rockefeller and the organizers of U.S. Steel. Paul de Kruif explains: "Alfred and Leonidas believed there was enough for everybody in those cut-throat business days of the 'nineties when men mostly succeeded because they knew there was never enough for one." Grant Merritt shares the belief of Alfred and Leonidas. People tend to be struck by Merritt's boyish face and restless energy, and not to notice that his eyes have the same dark, visionary intensity as the eyes of his ancestors.

In 1968, Merritt was co-chairman of the committee that was to draft the platform for the State Democratic–Farmer–Labor Party. He talked more about Reserve with his uncle Milton, and with scientists from the University of Minnesota (who were, he says, "inconclusive"). Then he drafted a platform plank that stated: "The use of Lake Superior as a dumping ground for mining or industrial wastes must be prohibited." The platform committee voted, 9–1, to adopt the plank, at a State convention bitterly divided over the war in Vietnam between supporters of two Minnesotans, Eugene McCarthy and Hubert Humphrey. The morning after the platform committee vote, Merritt recalls, he was summoned to the hotel room of a fellow Humphrey supporter, Congressman John Blatnik. Blatnik told him "I want that plank out of there." Blatnik recalls, "Merritt was sort of a neurotic to begin with. He said he didn't need scientific evidence." Merritt replies, "I've always said you should talk to those commercial fishermen who've fished the north shore for years before you talk to some of the scientists and engineers, because they have common sense and they can feel what's going on. They don't have degrees but they sure know what's happening and they knew it before anybody else did." Merritt refused Blatnik's request and the plank stayed in the platform.

In the meantime, Merritt began speaking out in public about Reserve Mining Company. His uncle had warned him that Stoddard's Taconite Study Group had done most of its water sampling while half of Reserve's plant was closed for regularly-scheduled maintenance. Merritt had written an open letter to Stoddard pointing this out, and he told reporters he feared Stoddard's study would be a "whitewash." (Merritt was delighted when his fears about Stoddard's report proved to be baseless; he says the report turned out to be "the key which opened this case to the public.") Merritt joined the Minnesota Environmental Control Citizen's Association (MECCA), an organization led mostly by young professional people concerned with environmental degradation in the Minneapolis–St. Paul area. "MECCA was a typical environmental point group," says a political reporter who covered them, "always heading off in all directions. Merritt was the most solid and stable guy they had." Merritt arrived in Duluth for the opening of the Lake Superior Enforcement Conference as Chairman of MECCA's Lake Superior Task Force.

In May of 1969 the citizen's movement to protect Lake Superior not only had an articulate and politically savvy spokesman in Grant Merritt, it also had an energetic practical organizer in Arlene Lind Harvell.

In February 1969, Grant Merritt's uncle Milton Mattson visited the Twin Points Resort, 10 miles down the lake shore from his home. He was looking for help from Arlene Lind Harvell's parents, who had bought this little resort when ill health forced Mr. Lind to leave Duluth during the Depression. John Lind was a long-time political activist. In the 20's and 30's, he had been a "Wobbly," a member of the radical-revolutionary Industrial Workers of the World. He still carried his red Wobbly card and wrote a regular column for the last surviving Wobbly newspaper, the Finnish-language *Industrialisti* in Duluth. Despite this background, he had not been a part of the supposed "Communist" effort to block Reserve Mining's original discharge permit; the State archives contain a 1947 petition *supporting* issuance of the permit, signed by Mr. Lind as secretary of the North Shore Resort Owners' Association. But his views had changed. Shortly after the release of Charles Stoddard's report in January 1969, Mr. Lind wrote to the *Duluth News-Tribune* that he and his wife dipped drinking water from a deep blue Lake Superior with buckets, when they first owned their resort; after Reserve Mining began production, the water flowing southwest past their resort turned a distinct greenish gray for a half mile off shore. "This greenish gray water I would term polluted, but having only a grade school education, company experts could probably convince me that the water is organically pure. But like the proverbial horse, they could lead me to that water, but they'd never again get me to drink it."

Milton Mattson talked to Mr. and Mrs. Lind about putting together an organization to fight the pollution of Lake Superior, but they turned him down. They were getting old, less able to bear the burden of organizing activity. Besides, with so many conservation organizations around, it didn't make sense to them to start another one. Hours after Mattson left the Twin Points Resort, Arlene Lind Harvell returned home from night classes at the University of Minnesota–Duluth. An attractive brunette, 29 years old, she had only recently moved back to Minnesota after the break-up of her marriage. She had taken her small son to play by the lake shore where she had played as a child. Like her father, she had been angered by the dirtying of the clear water of her youth. Because of their upbringing, Arlene recalls, the Lind children had always been "looked to as spokespeople" in school. She worked as a hairdresser during her marriage and held a number of offices in the hairdressers' organization. There, she recalls, she first experienced for herself the pervasive, often hidden, influence on American life of large corporations (in that case, the comestics industry).

When Mrs. Lind told her of Mattson's visit, Arlene said "I think you're wrong, Ma. The only way you'll get anything done is with an organization focussed on Lake Superior." Mrs. Lind telephoned Mattson and asked him to come back. He and Arlene Harvell sat in her room past midnight, planning the Save Lake Superior Association. Arlene got 18 people, all from along the North Shore, to attend an organizational meeting at the Twin Points Resort, where she was elected first president of the Save Lake Superior Association. Reserve was the major concern of these people, Arlene says, but "we tried to spread the blame" to include other pollution problems, such as shoreline development (especially nuclear power plants), shipboard wastes, and inadequate municipal sewage treatment. The Association decided to hold an educational program at the Two Harbors, Minnesota, high school. Arlene sent notices "all over" and the meeting drew people from as far away as Minneapolis–St. Paul and Ashland, Wisconsin. In April she organized chapters of the Save Lake Superior Association in Ashland and in Ironwood, Michigan, both focussed on local polluting industries. She and her mother designed "Save Lake Superior" campaign buttons and raised money by selling some 15,000 of them at 25 and 50 cents apiece. The Association searched out Dr. Louis Williams, who had first pursued Reserve as a scientist at the National Water Quality Laboratory. They found him at the University of Alabama and paid his airfare to Duluth so that he could present his findings at the first session of the Lake Superior Enforcement Conference. Arlene wrote to 16 organizations, such as the League of Women Voters and the Wisconsin Resource Conservation Council, urging them to speak at the conference. Representatives of 11 organizations attended a strategy meeting before the first session of the Conference, and provided speakers.

31

On the morning of May 13, 1969, several hundred people filled the ballroom of the Hotel Duluth to overflowing for the first session of the Lake Superior Enforcement Conference. Outside, 50 student members of the Save Lake Superior Association from Ashland High School picketed carrying anti-pollution "signs." Assistant Secretary of the Interior Carl Klein opened the session by outlining the legal basis for the conference; he informed the audience that the Federal government (and this conference) only had jurisdiction over sources of pollution which endangered the health or welfare of persons outside the State of origin. He then yielded the floor for a welcoming address by Congressman John Blatnik, who reiterated that, unless there was "scientific evidence on which to base a finding of interstate pollution," the discharge of Reserve Mining Company was solely within the jurisdiction of the State of Minnesota. Blatnik went on to assure the audience that "I obtained Federal authorization" for the National Water Quality Laboratory "on the shore of Lake Superior standing like a watchful, protective beacon. . . . With the help of the National Water Quality Laboratory, if there is pollution anywhere in Lake Superior, we are going to find it. And when we find it we are going to stop it." However, the opening speeches of Klein and Blatnik, stripped of their rhetorical flourishes, both carried the same message: the Lake Superior Enforcement Conference was powerless to deal with Reserve Mining Company's discharge, unless Reserve was causing pollution beyond the boundaries of Minnesota.

The business of the conference began with the submission of a report on water pollution in the Lake Superior basin by the regional office of the Federal Water Pollution Control Administration. This report discussed a number of industrial dischargers, including Reserve Mining Company. It softened the wording of Charles Stoddard's report on Reserve, but contained essentially the same conclusions — hardly surprising since it was the product of Donald Mount and the same administrative staff man who had helped him write the conclusions of Stoddard's report. But the report substituted for Stoddard's recommendation that Reserve be required to dispose of its tailings on land within three years a recommendation that the conferees keep the discharge "under continuing surveillance." The new report relied almost completely on the scientific work done for Stoddard's report. This caused some embarrassment, since the new Administration was determined not to give official recognition to Stoddard's report. Speakers who discussed the basis for the "official" report of the regional office had to resort to elaborate circumlocutions to avoid revealing that they were discussing the work which Stoddard had submitted to the Corps of Engineers as the basis of his summary report. Stoddard himself appeared uninvited at the conference, like Banquo's ghost, and tried without success to have his report made part of the record.

The Federal government did report three pieces of scientific research to the first session of the Lake Superior Enforcement Conference, in addition to those done for Stoddard's Taconite Study Group.

First, a hydraulic engineer testified that he had performed test tank experiments much like those performed for Reserve in 1947. While it could be predicted from these experiments that Reserve's tailings would form a density current in Lake Superior, it could also be predicted that the density current would be unstable, shedding clouds of fine tailings. Further, it could be predicted that a large part of the density current might be carried off into surface waters during the summer, when there would be a sharp division — called a thermocline — between the top layer of the lake heated by the sun, and the permanently cold deeper waters. (A team of student investigators later reported that in the original test tank experiments performed for Reserve, the tailings had been cold and the receiving water had been at room temperature — the reverse of actual operating conditions at Silver Bay. Such test conditions would have exaggerated the efficiency of the density current by increasing the relative density of the tailings effluent and decreasing the viscosity of the receiving water, thus decreasing the ability of the water to hold fine particles in suspension.)

Second, the director of the Interior Department laboratory in Lacrosse, Wisconsin, responded to Reserve's criticism of Stoddard's conclusion that diluted tailings could kill infant rainbow trout (namely, that rainbow trout spawn in streams, not in

Lake Superior). He reported that further tests showed 10 to one dilutions of tailings effluent were fatal to infant *lake* trout, as well as infant rainbow trout. However, his report also made clear, as the conclusions of Stoddard's report had not, that high concentrations of tailings did not kill older fish, or any other indicator organisms, in short-term tests.

Third, Donald Mount told the conference that the National Water Quality Laboratory had sampled municipal water systems along the Minnesota shore of Lake Superior during the winter. They had determined by x-ray diffraction analysis that samples of submicroscopic particles which had settled in the municipal water treatment basins of Beaver Bay, Two Harbors, and Duluth, Minnesota, contained concentrations of Reserve's tailings, declining from 85% to 10% with increasing distance from the discharge. They had also identified tailings in sediment samples siphoned from the bottoms of toilet flush tanks in the Duluth water distribution system more than 15 miles from the intake on the lake shore. They had taken these samples so that they could document the distribution of tailings in Lake Superior water, even though ice had closed the lake to navigation for the winter. No one claimed that the presence of Reserve's tailings in municipal water systems created any health hazard, although Federal witnesses pointed out that suspended particles do prolong the life of bacteria in water and do make the disinfection of drinking water more difficult.

The Wisconsin boundary is less than seven miles from the intake for the Duluth municipal water supply. Since the enforcement conference would not have jurisdiction to act on Reserve's discharge without evidence of interstate pollution, a conferee asked Mount if he had sampled beyond Minnesota waters for tailings. Mount's answer evaded the question. In fact, Mount and his staff had realized after finding substantial amounts of tailings in the Duluth water supply that the next step was to examine Wisconsin waters in order to establish interstate pollution. As soon as Lake Superior had been opened to navigation and a properly equipped boat had been available — just a week before the conference began — they had obtained dredge samples from the lake bottom within the boundaries of Wisconsin. And they had

34

identified tailings by x-ray diffraction in these samples. But Mount could not report these results. He had explained the results to Assistant Secretary Klein at the National Water Quality Laboratory the day before the conference began. To Mount's surprise, Klein exploded into a storm of table-pounding invective against Mount and his staff: under no circumstances were these results to be reported to the Lake Superior Enforcement Conference. Mount was not inclined to disobey Klein's order, but he had not previously made any attempt to keep the results of his Wisconsin sampling secret.

Assistant Secretary Klein left Duluth after opening the enforcement conference, leaving the Commissioner of the Federal Water Pollution Control Administration, David Dominick, in charge. Traditionally, relations are strained between Assistant Secretaries of the Interior, who try to lay down Department policy, and the heads of agencies and bureaus, with their own continuing problems and goals. In this case, there was also a deep personal antipathy. Klein referred to Dominick patronizingly as "the Kid." Dominick was only three years out of the University of Colorado Law School and he looked very young — short, clean shaven, wearing somewhat owlish glasses. Despite his youth, Dominick was inclined to be independent. An ex-Marine officer with a brusque, to-the-point manner of speaking, he wore cowboy boots and rolled his own cigarettes. In May 1969, Dominick recalls, his "sensitivities were heightened" by the recent *New York Times* description of his appointment as "undistinguished," "political," and "particularly disturbing." He now felt himself trapped between the personnel of his agency and a superior whom he was coming to regard as "something of a bully — a man of extraordinarily strong opinions and shallow knowledge."

On the first day of the conference, Grant Merritt approached Dominick in the dining room of the Hotel Duluth and handed him a letter. The letter was a demand under the Freedom of Information Act that the Federal government release the results of its analysis of Wisconsin samples. At the end of the day Dominick told Merritt he could go to the National Water Quality Laboratory and look at the results. At the beginning of the second day of the conference, a staff assistant read a message from Senator Gaylord

Nelson, which cited "reliable reports" that taconite tailings had been found in Wisconsin bottom samples. "This makes it clear that pollution of interstate waters is being caused by Reserve Mining Company's tailings disposal at Silver Bay," Nelson's message stated, "and settles the dispute over whether this conference has jurisdiction over Reserve's operation. It would be unfortunate if, with the evidence and with the authorities available, the conferees were to accept a recommendation calling only for continued surveillance."

During a recess in the conference, Ron Way, the Minneapolis reporter who had broken the story of Stoddard's report, saw Congressman Blatnik, David Dominick and Donald Mount enter an unused barroom of the Hotel Duluth. Way was immediately suspicious, since he knew the rumors that Blatnik wielded his considerable political influence to protect Reserve. Poking around a back hall, Way found a service entrance to the room, eased the door open, and crept on his hands and knees under the bar where the three men sat talking. It was clear, he says, that "Blatnik was calling the shots — he was dictating terms to these guys." Blatnik recalls he thought that Mount wanted to use his findings "just as a technicality," that the findings were "premature." Dominick concedes, "As a young administrator with only a few months on the job, I was quite respectful of Mr. Blatnik. He was the chairman of our subcommittee and there were a lot of things the agency needed from Congress." After the recess, the three men acted out the scenario devised by Blatnik in the barroom: Dominick called on Blatnik to speak; Blatnik in turn said that someone from the National Water Quality Laboratory should deal with the question of Wisconsin samples; Mount then stood up and explained that his laboratory had found cummingtonite-grunerite in Wisconsin bottom samples, but would need to do more work before identifying Reserve Mining Company as the source.

Reserve's original lawyer, William K. Montague, attended the Lake Superior Enforcement Conference, but the company's case was presented by Montague's young partner, Edward T. Fride. A trial lawyer with quick brown eyes and the solid build of a football player, Fride had a sense of the dramatic and an instinct for the jugular. He tirelessly reiterated the company's story at every opportunity, in speeches, arguments and affidavits. He told how Reserve's operation had been encouraged and duly authorized by responsible State and Federal agencies. How first one and then another publicity-seeking zealot (Louis Williams and Charles Stoddard) misled public opinion and aroused it against Reserve's operation. How politicians eager to placate voters organized the massive machinery of the Federal government against this single company, ignoring its lawful permits, pressuring responsible scientists into unwarranted claims of harm. At the May 1969 session of the Lake Superior Enforcement Conference Fride presented testimony on behalf of Reserve that was to be repeated many times without basic change in the succeeding years. Edward Schmid, Reserve's chief public relations officer and a former Armco Steel executive, testified that Reserve's tailings discharge formed a "heavy density current" which "flows down into the very deepest place in the area . . . the Great Trough," where "the fine particles settle out. That is where they are supposed to go, according to our permits and to all scientific predictions. Our extensive bottom sampling program proves that is where they are going." Reserve's president Edward Furness, a former Republic Steel executive, testified that cummingtonite-grunerite by itself "is not a valid indicator of tailings." He went on: "Tailings are pure sand . . . . They are inert, inorganic, insoluble in Lake Superior, and biologically inactive . . . . There is no material discoloration of the water and the turbidity has not been adversely affected by Reserve's operations." Schmid elaborated: "if green water were caused by Reserve's tailings discharge — and it is *not* — you would expect to see it near Silver Bay constantly. You don't." Kenneth Haley, Reserve's Vice President for Research and Development, a former executive of Armco Steel, testified that the work of the Federal Water Pollution Control Administration, given proper statistical treatment, "shows that, from a chemical and turbidity standpoint, the water in the Silver Bay area has higher purity than the balance of the lake . . . ." Furness testified that the company discharged tailings into Lake Superior only because they had to. They had wanted to locate their plant near their mine on the Mesabi Range, but they had been forced to Silver Bay because the area near Babbitt, Minnesota, lacked enough water for their concentrating operation and suitable land for tailings disposal. Furness also testified that work by engineering consultants showed the adoption of Charles Stoddard's recommendation to dispose of Reserve's tailings on land near Silver Bay would cost the company some $195 million to $253 million in capital — and an additional $2.50 to $2.75 per ton of iron pellets produced.

The company's presentation was supported by the work of a number of specially-hired consultants — among them Leon Weinberger and Max Edwards, who had expressed the previous Administration's official disapproval of the work of Louis Williams and Charles Stoddard. Reserve's chief scientific consultant was G. Fred Lee, a professor of water chemistry at the University of Wisconsin — a man with an aura of impregnable self-confidence. Lee had been a consultant to the Federal Water Pollution Control Administration in September 1968, when he had been asked to Duluth to help the agency's regional office prepare its report on water quality for Stoddard's Taconite Study Group. He had found an important weakness in the report: biologists were mainly concerned about the effects of dissolved chemicals in water; but the regional office had analyzed its samples without filtering them, so that it obtained a single figure for the amount of each chemical in a water sample, whether the chemical was actually dissolved or only present in suspended particles. In October Lee had written to Reserve, pointing this out as a possible response to Stoddard's conclusion that Reserve was exceeding the accepted criteria for certain chemicals in water. He had also offered the company his services as a consultant and they had accepted. Lee first charged Reserve $150 a day (plus expenses), then $200, then $300, for consulting services that included advice on legal and technical strategy, suggestions for Reserve's sampling program, recommendations on equipment, the hiring of additional consultants in oceanography, mineralogy and micro-biology, and coordination of their work. Lee testified that scientists who opposed Reserve's discharge were "intentionally distorting the information available" to them. At the same time he wrote to Reserve's public relations office that he had addressed scientific groups on the Reserve problem: "I believe that . . . I was able to convince a substantial number of them . . . that the alleged effects of the discharge of taconite tailings on water quality were largely of political origin rather than technical. I almost had Reserve management wearing 'white hats' again . . . . I wish to mention that if the honorarium is right, I would give consideration to giving this talk in Silver Bay." While serving as a consultant to several other firms and as a fulltime member of the University of Wisconsin faculty, Lee collected $135,000 from Reserve over the next five years. Over the same period, Reserve paid an additional $80,000 to the University of Wisconsin to support work performed by a doctoral candidate under Lee's supervision; in return, Lee assigned the candidate to work closely with Reserve on the effects of taconite tailings and gave his thesis to Reserve for editorial deletions and corrections before submitting it for academic review. Professor Lee summarized his testimony to the Lake Superior Enforcement Conference: "The only potential adverse effect of this firm's discharge is that it may increase the frequency of green water in the region of Silver Bay, Minnesota."

Citizen organizations were active throughout the Lake Superior Enforcement Conference. Edward Fride marshalled business groups such as the Northeastern Minnesota Development Association and the Duluth Area Chamber of Commerce and a number of local governments in support of Reserve's position. For example, the mayor of Babbitt, Minnesota, testified that "it is not consistent with Reserve policies, as we know them, to overlook any phase of our community's health and welfare." Citizen opposition to Reserve coalesced around the Northern Environmental Council, an umbrella organization formed by Charles Stoddard, Grant Merritt and Arlene Harvell, after the first session of the conference. Their Council eventually included MECCA, the Save Lake Superior Association, United Northern Sportsmen, the Wisconsin Resource Conservation Council, the Duluth Chapter of the Izaak Walton League and more than two dozen other groups. Working out of office space donated by Stoddard, the Northern Environmental Council raised money, prepared studies, and coordinated positions on Reserve Mining and other conservation issues in the Lake Superior area. The Council and its member organizations were hampered by a chronic shortage of funds, but they nevertheless played an effective role.

The Lake Superior Enforcement Conference met twice each year during 1969, 1970 and 1971. The conference adopted abatement schedules for dozens of industrial and municipal discharges into Lake Superior and its tributaries. But most of the time of the conference was occupied by protracted consideration of a single discharge, that of Reserve Mining Company. State and Federal officials at the conference were always asking for more evidence on the points that Reserve had put in issue. "I, for one, would not like the record to stand that as conferees we are waiting for a dead body to be floating in Wisconsin waters," said Michigan's representative in 1970. But, he added, he was still "waiting for some good solid information" on which to act. If the citizens grouped around the Northern Environmental Council could not afford detailed scientific and engineering studies, they could offer testimony that concentrated the attention of officials at the enforcement conference on the forest rather than the trees. Pollution, they told the conferees, was scientifically defined as "any intrusion of foreign matter or energy into a natural ecological system." Under any scientific definition, Reserve was polluting Lake Superior. Reserve's tailings could not properly be described as sand, since texts on sedimentation define sand particles as being 2 millimeters to 1/16 millimeter in diameter, and Reserve's own tests showed that most of the tailings were much finer — in the silt and clay size ranges. Nor could the tailings be described as inert, since there are no insoluble materials, only relatively insoluble ones; and the solubility of materials increases as they are divided into finer sizes. The Minnesota Pollution Control Agency was giving Reserve unequal treatment, since it required other taconite producers on the Mesabi Iron Range to operate closed systems for tailings disposal, in order to avoid polluting nearby lakes. The very existence of such disposal systems demonstrated their engineering and economic feasibility. In any case, when the conference judged Reserve's financial capability to adopt a closed system of on-land disposal, it should remember that Reserve was not an independent company; it never sold any of its product, but delivered equal shares to Armco and Republic Steel; Reserve was a subsidiary, operated as a division of Armco and Republic — corporations with a total of more than $75 million a year of retained net income.

But the most important message of citizen organizations to the Lake Superior Enforcement Conference was not in the field of science, or engineering, or economics. Their message was philosophical and political. These citizens of Minnesota and Wisconsin and Michigan treasured the unspoiled beauty of Lake Superior. Arlene Harvell told the conference that the democratic system must take into consideration the thousands of citizens who had arisen to to say "No, we don't want that use made of the lake any more. We are sorry, but we have changed our minds." Grant Merritt offered a citizen affidavit which said: "Even my daughter can recognize this kind of pollution and realize that it must be stopped. Would I permit her to wipe her muddy feet on a clean blue carpet? No more readily will I stand by and allow taconite tailings to soil Lake Superior without protest." The conferees and some conservationists agonized indecisively over what to do about Reserve, but the members of the Northern Environmental Council consistently offered one solution: "total on-land disposal . . . . We will not accept any disposal plan which uses the lake as a tailings basin . . . . We will accept no compromise." A conferee asked Grant Merritt if MECCA took the position that: "as a means of preserving the integrity of Lake Superior . . . whatever the environmental price might be for onshore disposal, it is a tolerable price?" And Merritt replied: "That is correct. This is precisely right."

According to a considerable body of academic opinion, the unswerving insistence of the Northern Environmental Council that Reserve be prohibited from discharging *any* tailings into Lake Superior was extreme and simplistic. Such academicians dismiss the conviction that some things are worth preserving no matter what the price as romantic, quasi-religious. They argue that the government should not take any action without a cool-headed, pragmatic assessment of the costs and benefits of that action. For example, Dr. Alfred E. Kahn, a leading regulatory economist, has written:

> [O]ur total resources, including our environmental resources, are insufficient to permit us to do and have everything that we would like to do and have. The fundamental economic problem, therefore, is one of making the best possible choices; . . . the extent to which we pursue our environmental goals must . . . be subjected to the same kind of economic — i.e. cost/ benefit — tests as the extent to which we supply the people of this country with food, housing, medical care, museums, education, and police and fire protection . . . . Only . . . so long as pollution abatement is less costly than pollution should it be adopted . . . .
>
> [A] zero discharge goal . . . is simply irrational. It places an absolute priority on this single environmental goal . . . without considering whether beyond some point the costs of bringing discharges another step closer to zero might far exceed the additional benefits of doing so.

Environmentalists have learned to play the academic economist's game, however. They point out that there is no agreed method for placing a monetary value on many things in life, conceding for the moment that it would be desirable to do so. Consequently, environmental cost/benefit analyses often only add an elaborate layer of pseudo-science over the basic, subjective value judgments that people start with. Eventually, the citizens groups in the Northern Environmental Council found economists who would place a sufficiently high value on the benefits to be derived from protecting Lake Superior to justify almost any cost for on-land disposal.

The first session of the Lake Superior Enforcement Conference adjourned on May 15, 1969, without taking action. The conferees met again on September 30, 1969. At that time, Donald Mount reported that the National Water Quality Laboratory had taken further samples and could now identify Reserve Mining

Company as the source of cummingtonite-grunerite found in Wisconsin "beyond a shadow of a doubt." The conferees easily adopted "mom-and-apple-pie" conclusions proposed by the regional office of the Federal Water Pollution Control Administration that the esthetic value and deep blue appearance of Lake Superior were of major importance and that "Lake Superior is a priceless natural heritage which the present generation holds in trust for posterity, with an obligation to pass it on in the best possible condition." Michigan's representative, supported by Wisconsin's, proposed that the Conference conclude: "There is presumptive evidence in the record to indicate that the discharges from the Reserve Mining Company endanger the health or welfare of persons" outside Minnesota. His proposal was accepted. Finally, the conferees agreed to scrap the old Federal proposal that the conference limit its action to keeping Reserve under continued surveillance. Instead, they recommended that Reserve be asked to report, within six months of the Interior Secretary's approval of their recommendation, on engineering and economic studies of "means of reducing by the maximum practicable extent the discharge of tailings to Lake Superior." The report was to "include a tentative timetable for necessary action."

Within a week of this action, Armco Steel's chief environmental officer was urging "vigorous political activity, primarily in Washington, D.C.," to convince Secretary Hickel that he should modify the conclusions and recommendations of the conference. David Dominick does not recall any political pressures at this time, although he says he probably discussed the conclusions and recommendations with Congressman Blatnik. Dominick says that Assistant Secretary Klein, "a massive wheeler and dealer, . . . probably would have gotten any political heat on Reserve." Donald Mount was called to Washington in December 1969 to brief Secretary Hickel. He recalls being warned cryptically by Carl Klein at the time, that "We don't want to embarrass our President." "It was hard to know just what Klein thought," Mount says. "He seemed to just want the problem to go away." In January 1970, Secretary Hickel formally acted on the conclusions and recommendations of the Lake Superior Enforcement Conference. Hickel, a spirited politican and a shrewd judge of public

43

opinion, was then one year into his tireless campaign to convert initially-hostile conservationists into supporters. He approved the conclusions and recommendations of the conference.

During 1969, Reserve Mining Company spent approximately $325,000 on lawyers and consultants to defend itself. And Reserve returned approximately $17,500,000 in after-tax profits to Armco and Republic Steel.

III

The Deep Pipe

After the first session of the Lake Superior Enforcement Conference ended in 1969, Commissioner Dominick of the Federal Water Pollution Control Administration asked Donald Mount of the National Water Quality Laboratory to tell him what further studies were needed to establish the effects of Reserve Mining Company's discharge on Lake Superior. Mount sat down to plan the work with several members of his staff. The most enthusiastic of them was an ebullient 28-year old chemist, Dr. Gary Glass.

Gary Glass was born in Duluth and raised on Park Point — a long sandspit, less than a block wide, which separates Duluth harbor from Lake Superior. He grew up beachcombing the shore of the lake but had no strong feeling that the environment needed protecting. From grade school on, Glass was preoccupied with making rockets, jet engines, and carbide cannons. (His favorite holiday was the 4th of July.) His ambition was "to play with science." He married the girl next door, Fayth Carlson, and left Duluth to attend graduate school. He went to work at the National Water Quality Laboratory in 1968, because it was an opportunity both to return to his hometown and to do useful scientific work. Glass is a controversial figure among his colleagues at the laboratory, but they all agree that he is a bright, inventive, articulate, intensely ambitious perfectionist who drives himself and others hard. Glass was enthusiastic about working on Reserve's discharge, because, he says, it was the laboratory's biggest project and it had practical application to the largest body of freshwater in the country. His father-in-law had given him a tour of the Reserve plant a few years before and he'd been impressed, but hadn't really thought about pollution.

Mount, Glass, and their colleagues worked out a plan, including time and cost estimates, for their laboratory and others in the agency to perform studies aimed at answering basic questions about the distribution of Reserve's tailings in Lake Superior and their impact on water quality and aquatic organisms. Mount sent the plan to Washington via the regional office of the Federal Water Pollution Control Administration. Weeks went by. Mount heard nothing. Finally, he called Washington and got back a memo directing him to proceed with those studies which only the National Water Quality Laboratory could perform. There was no mention of costs. Mount called Washington again to ask if any money would be provided. He got another memo directing him to cover costs by taking money from his national research program, without giving up any element of that program. In a large and impersonal bureaucracy, where personal contact is often reduced to telephone calls and memos, many people measure sincerity and depth of conviction in dollars and cents. Mount was left to conclude that his superiors were sincere and deeply convinced about abating Reserve Mining Company's discharge, only if it didn't cost them anything.

During 1969-1970, Mount scrounged enough money from his regular research budget to perform a few laboratory studies that responded to Dominick's request. Gary Glass prepared reports on the causes of "green water," on the dissolution of tailings, and on the effects of tailings on algae growth. Mount presented these reports and three others at the April 1970 session of the Lake Superior Enforcement Conference. He said the reports not only showed "beyond reasonable doubt" that Reserve caused bands of green water in Lake Superior, they also showed that Reserve contributed material quantities of dissolved materials to the lake and promoted the growth of both algae and bacteria. He emphasized to the conferees that, "The discharge is one of many sources increasing the dissolved materials in the water and these materials provide some acceleration of the lake's aging process." The studies lessened Mount's initial skepticism; he later recalled that "the nutrient effect was one which I did not even consider originally."

The enforcement conference met again in August 1970. Murray Stein had chaired each session of the conference since the first one, but it was clear by this time that Donald Mount was dominating the proceedings. The atmosphere of the conference was emotionally charged. But Mount's scientific reputation was beyond dispute — even Reserve's consultant, G. Fred Lee, conceded that he was "one of the top three people in the world in the area of aquatic toxicology." Mount delivered his carefully-worded statements without bravado or rhetorical flourishes. The politicians at the conference seized on him as a neutral scientific refuge from conflicting pressures. At the August session, Michigan's representative asked Mount the ultimate legal question: was the discharge of Reserve Mining Company part of a total contribution to Lake Superior that endangered the health or welfare of persons in Michigan or Wisconsin? Mount replied: "Well, I would not have been quite so positive about that some months ago, but . . . I think there is a clear endangerment of the use of this lake." He elaborated: "This conference decided that the lake's beauty was to be protected and the quality of the lake preserved. As Lake Superior ages, its present quality will degrade in contradiction to the goals set forth by this conference." He outlined the effects of eutrophication, or aging: a reduction in water clarity from biological growth, nuisance problems from the overabundance of algae, and shifts in kinds of fish. "Of course these changes are not yet in evidence in Lake Superior, but when the changes can be seen the damage will have been inflicted. Once these persistent materials are added to Lake Superior and become incorporated in it, the removal with present or foreseeable technology will not be possible and they will be there, for all practical purposes permanently . . . so it will be imperative to use predictive means whenever possible." The studies of the National Water Quality Laboratory provided these predictive means.

Following Mount's statement, the Lake Superior Enforcement Conference unanimously adopted the conclusion that "there is evidence in the record to indicate that the dischargers named by the conferees in their reports to the conference, including the

Reserve Mining Company, endanger the health or welfare of persons in states other than that in which such discharges originate." Reserve had presented the April session of the enforcement conference with 19 engineering studies of ways to change the company's discharge into Lake Superior. The company had labelled most of the studies as of "questionable feasibility." They had presented no timetable for abatement. The conferees now adopted another recommendation that Reserve provide them "a specified method for abating its discharge to Lake Superior, which will meet State and Federal requirements" by December 1, 1970. Wisconsin's representative explained his support for this recommendation: "we were particularly impressed by the public value on Lake Superior. And that value, it seems to us, is to maintain it in its pristine purity and minimize the aging process of the lake."

While the Lake Superior Enforcement Conference was meeting, Reserve was entangled in a complicated court case with the State of Minnesota. In the fall of 1969, the Sierra Club sued the State's Republican administration to force them to hold hearings on the revocation of Reserve's 1947 permit. A State district court judge in Minneapolis issued a writ of mandamus requiring the State to hold the hearings. A second Minneapolis judge affirmed this order. On Christmas Eve 1969, Reserve Mining Company counterattacked by suing the State before C. Luther Eckman, a State district court judge for Lake County, the site of its plant. Reserve asked Judge Eckman to enjoin the permit revocation hearings ordered by the Minneapolis judges, and to grant it an exemption from the water quality standards that had just been adopted by the State and approved by Secretary Hickel. Judge Eckman granted an injunction against the permit hearings and set the question of an exemption from water quality standards down for trial. The second Minneapolis judge acceded to Judge Eckman's injunction "with great reluctance." But the Republican administration, baited by Grant Merritt and his allies in the Democratic-Farmer-Labor Party, counter-sued Reserve before Judge Eckman, asking that he order the company to comply with the State's water quality standards.

Less than three weeks before the trial began, a State assistant attorney general visited Donald Mount to ask for scientific help in preparing for trial. Mount turned to Gary Glass, who quickly accepted the job. For the next three months Glass put in 12- and 16-hour days, combing files, finding Federal and academic scientists to serve as witnesses and preparing lawyers for cross-examinations — much the same job that G. Fred Lee was performing for Reserve. His work did not escape Lee's attention. Lee wrote to Donald Mount that "the reputation of your laboratory has been damaged by . . . your 'Save Lake Superior chemist.' "

The result of Glass' work was a large body of evidence, hotly contested by Reserve, that the company was polluting Lake Superior and contributing to its eutrophication. Donald Mount says "Without Gary, the State's case couldn't have lasted three days." Glass enjoyed the work: "it was like being a ring-master in a circus — you could construct a whole show . . . . I didn't know I was capable of being an operator, but it came naturally." As a Federal employee, Glass was prohibited from taking any additional compensation for his work. In fact, Mount says, the months Glass spent working for the State Attorney General were irrelevant to his professional career — a delay in climbing the promotion ladder. But Fayth Glass enthusiastically supported her husband's work. She attended the trial and, during a recess one day, met with Arlene Harvell in the ladies room to join the Save Lake Superior Association.

The chief frustration of Glass' job was Judge Eckman's apparent inability to grasp scientific issues: three weeks into the trial, the Judge interrupted testimony about the eutrophication of Lake Superior to ask, "Is that putrefication or putrefaction?" As a back-up to scientific evidence, Glass had a co-worker at the National Water Quality Laboratory drive along the lake shore every day looking for a "really gross" occurrence of green water — something, Glass says, the Judge simply couldn't ignore. One morning, the man called to tell Glass excitedly that there was "green water all over the western end of the lake." Judge Eckman was taken to a waiting Minnesota Highway Patrol plane by the State attorneys. Glass recalls that Judge Eckman motioned Reserve's lawyer Edward Fride to the bench the morning after he flew over the lake, and said "Gee, Ed, it was really bad out there yesterday."

On December 15, 1970, Judge Eckman handed down his decision. He wrote:

> The Court, completely lacking in personal expertise, found itself in the impossible position of being required to analyze, weigh, and choose between . . . controversial points of view . . . . [T]he Court would be indulging in speculation to make a determination that the discharge was or was not a potential source of pollution to Lake Superior.

But Judge Eckman did find that Reserve's discharge had resulted in an "increase of the 'green water phenomenon' " and he went on:

> [E]ven though there has been no substantial or convincing evidence of deterioration to date, the Court cannot disregard the numerous scientific opinions expressed to the effect that the present method of discharge constitutes a possible or potential source of pollution which, if continued over a long period of time, might result in the material deterioration of the water quality of Lake Superior.

Although the Judge ordered the State to excuse Reserve from conforming with Federally-approved water quality standards, he also ordered Reserve to modify its method of discharge. He wrote that: "any modification must insure the flocculation of the fine tailings and the deposit of all the tailings by conduit to the floor of the great trough where they will remain, eliminating thereby their dispersion to other parts of Lake Superior."

Less than one month before Judge Eckman handed down his decision, the Reserve Mining Company board of directors had met at Cleveland, Ohio, the corporate home of Republic Steel, and voted to adopt the very modifications that the Judge was shortly to order. They had endorsed one of the 19 plans that Reserve had presented to the April session of the Lake Superior Enforcement Conference. Under this plan, the tailings would be discharged into large conical settling tanks on Reserve's delta, and organic chemicals, called flocculants, would be added which would change the electric charge on the surface of the tailings particles, binding them loosely into large flattened clumps like wet snowflakes. Over-flow water from the tanks would run into Lake Superior near the plant's water intake. The underflow — that is the water drained from the bottom of these cones — would contain about 40% flocculated tailings by weight, contrasted with 1.4% tailings in the existing discharge; this under-flow would be piped below the surface of the lake. (When the plan was presented at the conference, Reserve's consulting engineer was asked why it was necessary to thicken the discharge stream of tailings. He said, "The minute you begin to increase the volume of water to dilute it, you tend to create problems of turbulence which results in further turbidity," thus dealing an inadvertant back-hand blow to Reserve's claims for the efficiency of its existing "heavy density current.") The tailings piped 150-feet deep into the lake would fall 600 feet to the bottom and slowly pile up. Since shallower bottom areas generally support more aquatic life than deeper bottom areas, Reserve presented its plan optimistically as an "Under-water Sand Reef Beneficial to Bottom Fauna and Fish."

During 1970, Reserve Mining Company spent approximately $700,000 on lawyers and consultants to defend itself. And Reserve returned approximately $20,000,000 in after-tax profits to Armco and Republic Steel.

At the end of 1970, Donald Mount recalls, he was visiting relatives in Miami, when he got a phone call from Reserve's lawyer, Edward Fride. Fride was with Murray Stein, who was vacationing at Lauderdale-by-the-Sea. Could Mount come up? Mount had no car, but Fride would pay for a cab. (Mount recalls being a little awe-struck when Fride kept the cabdriver waiting during their meeting and gave him a handful of cash — he wasn't used to seeing that kind of money.) At Lauderdale-by-the-Sea, Fride and Reserve's public relations director, Edward Schmid, gave Stein and Mount copies of Judge Eckman's decision and presented the deep pipe disposal plan, complete with three-dimensional model. Stein and Mount indicated informally that "the plan looked promising — this sort of thing should be acceptable to the Federal government." Stein agreed to present the plan to the next session of the Lake Superior Enforcement Conference in January 1971. At this point, Stein and Mount recall, they had no dramatic evidence of degraded water quality, the State trial had been lost despite Federal help, and Reserve showed no inclination to do anything else. In addition, Stein was under pressure to produce some short-term results, because another reorganization of the Federal government's pollution control activities was underway.

Secretary of the Interior Walter Hickel had followed his instinct for popular politics too far. On April 30, 1970, President Nixon had ordered the invasion of Cambodia. A wave of protests, often violent, followed on the nation's college campuses. Even after four students were killed at Kent State University, the President maintained a hostile attitude toward student protests. Hickel, distressed that Nixon was throwing away the youthful enthusiasm he'd been trying to channel into work on the environment, wrote a letter to Nixon warning him that, "if we read history, it clearly shows that youth in its protest must be heard." The letter was leaked to the press almost as soon as it was sent, and Hickel was a marked man in the Administration. Nixon had on his desk a recommendation from a hand-picked commission that the Federal government's pollution fighting activities be centralized within the Department of the Interior, which already included the Federal Water Pollution Control Administration. Nixon reversed this recommendation and announced in June 1970 that all Interior's pollution control activities would be transferred to a new, independent Environmental Protection Agency (EPA). A loyal Nixon assistant explained somewhat delicately that the effect of Hickel's letter on Nixon had been "to confirm his opinion that Hickel — who had allowed the leak, either on purpose or inadvertently — was a poor manager." The night before Thanksgiving 1970, with the mid-term Congressional elections safely out of the way, Nixon called Hickel to the White House and fired him. The day after Thanksgiving, a Presidential assistant went to the Department of the Interior and fired Hickel's personal staff at the Office of the Secretary from the government; he told them to clean out their desks and be gone by the end of the day.

The Environmental Protection Agency began operations in December 1970. The new agency's Administrator was William Ruckelshaus, a large, amiable man in his late thirties, his dark hair, square jaw and horn-rimmed glasses making him a double for earnest, reliable Clark Kent. After running unsuccessfully as the Republican candidate for the United States Senate from Indiana in 1968, Ruckelshaus had been appointed an Assistant Attorney General of the United States. His boss, John N. Mitchell, had secured the Administrator's job for him. Ruckelshaus briefly considered Murray Stein for the combined job of Assistant Administrator for Enforcement and General Counsel of EPA, but settled instead on a Harvard Law School contemporary, John Quarles, a slight, bookish assistant to Walter Hickel. Quarles had given notice that he was leaving Hickel's staff the day before Hickel was fired; when Quarles had arrived at the staff offices of the Secretary of the Interior the Monday after Thanksgiving, his was the only name left on the wall directory. "I assumed," he has said, "that I had been passed over partly because I was moving to EPA."

Hickel remained adamant for his own particular brand of political independence, even after his firing. He wrote in his memoir *Who Owns America?*:

'Politics is the art of compromise.' If those words were carved out of solid granite in ten-foot high letters up each side of the Washington Monument, they would be no more revered than they already are in the American capital. The expression has been used for generations as an excuse for selling out one's beliefs and 'making a deal.' The man who listens, who finds out the naked truth and goes forward without compromise, is a truly great leader.

But Hickel's experience at the Department of the Interior had the opposite effect on John Quarles, whose name was to become a byword for caution at EPA. In *Cleaning Up America*, Quarles writes that he warned Ruckelshaus:

Bill, you and I come from the opposite ends of the earth in this regard. You've been at the Justice Department, where John Mitchell sits at the right hand of the President and his subordinates can do no wrong. I was at Interior, where Wally Hickel had no strength in the White House at all and we were constantly being sniped at by everyone in the White House and OMB [the Office of Management and Budget]. You have to strike a balance. If you get those fellows turned against you, the agency will suffer in ways we can't even foresee.

Quarles writes that, despite his advice, William Ruckelshaus decided at the outset to tie "the fortunes of EPA to public opinion as the only base of political support . . . . The environmental movement demanded strong action and EPA responded to the pressures of the grassroots political protest in all the decisions and actions initiated by Bill Ruckelshaus as Administrator. The response was reflected most clearly in his approach to enforcement." Ruckelshaus himself says "we needed to establish our willingness to enforce standards. I hoped that a few well-publicized cases would lead businessmen to conclude that they should comply voluntarily." Ruckelshaus sent a staff assistant to the January 1971 session of the Lake Superior Enforcement Conference in Duluth, to see how well Murray Stein fitted this strategy. Stein's career in the bureaucracy was already declining. A few months earlier, Stein had reported directly to the head of his agency. Now he had to report through John Quarles. Within another few months, he would have to report through Quarles' deputy.

The night before the conference reopened, Donald Mount called Charles Stoddard to his home to meet with Murray Stein. As the man behind the Northern Environmental Council, Stoddard was crucial to public acceptance of any enforcement conference action. Stoddard recalls that Stein pleaded, "I've got to settle. This case has dragged on too long." He laid out the deep pipe proposal. Mount and Gary Glass had just visited Reserve's R & D lab at Silver Bay for a demonstration of the proposal. Mount had made a friendly bet that the deep pipe would work as described;

he was cautiously optimistic, while Glass thought "it was a crock." Mount's main concern was the addition of an organic flocculant to the discharge. As he told the conference later, either the flocculant would break down, causing oxygen depletion in settled tailings on the bottom of the lake, and the leaching of more dissolved metals from the tailings into the lake water; or it would not break down, and there would be a new persistent organic compound in the lake to worry about. Charles Stoddard listened to Stein and Mount, then said so far as he was concerned "it was no go."

On January 14, 1971, Stein reopened the Lake Superior Enforcement Conference. He read a short letter from William Ruckelshaus: previous sessions of the conference had approved abatement timetables for dozens of industrial dischargers to Lake Superior, but Reserve Mining Company was still under no deadline; "I feel that this special consideration of one polluter must end." Stein called on Edward Fride, who said that Reserve was ready to begin work now on the deep pipe proposal. Edward Furness, Reserve's president, explained that the company had put forward this proposal "not because we believed our present operations were harming or threatening Lake Superior in any way, but because we were anxious to relieve the concern some people have about Reserve's use of the lake." He outlined the proposal, which, he said, would cost Reserve approximately $14 million in capital, with a total cost of about 25¢ per ton of annual iron pellet production. Citizen activists were not moved by the company's presentation. Stein argued that rejection of the deep pipe proposal could lead to another two years of delay, during which Reserve would continue dumping 67,000 tons of taconite tailings into Lake Superior every day. A staff member of the Northern Environmental Council replied that, if the deep pipe proposal were adopted, "this dumping into the lake will not go on for two years but for 42."

Citizen activists were in a much stronger political position at this session of the enforcement conference than they had been in August. They now counted on the support of the newly-elected Democratic governors of Minnesota and Wisconsin. Wendell R. Anderson of Minnesota, a strikingly handsome alumnus of

America's 1956 Olympic hockey team, had been one of only a handful of DFL legislators who had opposed the Taconite Amendment to the State Constitution in 1964. Anderson says, "a constitution is a place where you guarantee things like individuals' freedom of speech and freedom of religion, not corporations' freedom from taxation." After Grant Merritt had addressed the first session of the Lake Superior Enforcement Conference in May 1969, Anderson invited him to lunch and asked him to draft two bills — one placing a stiff tax on the dumping of mining wastes into Lake Superior, and the other prohibiting the dumping altogether. Anderson introduced these bills in the Minnesota legislature. When Anderson announced his candidacy for governor in the 1970 election, Merritt was the first DFL congressional district chairman to endorse him. During the campaign, Anderson had addressed the August 1970 session of the enforcement conference. In every county in Minnesota, he told the conferees, he had heard from the people, young and old, of their concern for the environment: "They want tough, fair and firm action and they want it now . . . . I hope . . . that a specific timetable will be established for the total cessation of dumping of taconite tailings in Lake Superior by December 31 of 1972." The same day Minnesota elected Anderson governor, Wisconsin elected as its governor Patrick J. Lucey, who had been the liberal chairman of the State Democratic Party during Gaylord Nelson's administration. Lucey was a friend of Charles Stoddard.

On the morning the two new governors spoke before the January 1971 session of the Lake Superior Enforcement Conference, Merritt and Stoddard briefed them about the deep pipe. In his speech, Governor Anderson reiterated the position he had taken as a candidate; he "never seriously considered the deep pipe," he recalls. Governor Lucey urged the conference to take "bold steps . . . no halfway measures." So there would be no mistake about his position, Lucey sent a telegram to the conference the next day declaring "Under no circumstances will I support the underwater disposal plan." He called for "an in-depth study of land disposal . . . by an unbiased committee within 60 days." The most Murray Stein could do in the face of the governors' opposition was to get the conference to recess while a technical committee considered both on-land disposal and the deep pipe.

William Ruckelshaus recalls that the assistant he sent out to check on progress at the January 1971 session of the Lake Superior Enforcement Conference, "didn't think much of it." David Dominick was now a part of EPA, with the temporary title of Acting Commissioner, Water Quality Office, pending his appointment as assistant administrator in charge of another part of the agency. He asked Ruckelshaus if he could go to Duluth to chair the enforcement conference when it reconvened. "I had a personal interest in the disposition of the Reserve matter," he recalls. "It was one of EPA's major bits of unfinished business from the Federal Water Pollution Control Administration . . . . Some senior person had to represent the agency, to try to bring the case to some formal conclusion." Ruckelshaus agreed to send Dominick. During March, Dominick met with John Quarles and with Ruckelshaus. On paper at least, Quarles was in charge of enforcement at EPA, but Dominick managed to dodge his repeated requests for some description of what he planned to do about Reserve.

On April 21, 1971, David Dominick returned to the Hotel Duluth, where two years before he had jumped through hoops for Carl Klein and John Blatnik. He called Grant Merritt to his room. Now Merritt was not simply an interested citizen, but an official representative of the State of Minnesota entitled to participate in the decisions of the enforcement conference. Governor Anderson had just appointed him Executive Director of the Minnesota Pollution Control Agency. A month earlier, the officers of Armco, Republic, and Reserve had held a gloomy discussion in Chicago of Merritt's pending appointment. It was the consensus of their meeting that Merritt could only create mischief for them. They did find hope in the report that Senator Humphrey and Congressman Blatnik were urging Governor Anderson not to appoint him. Anderson says, "I would certainly recall any pressure from my good friend, Hubert Humphrey, not to appoint Grant. There just wasn't any." As executive director, Merritt was reshaping the Pollution Control Agency in his aggressive image. He secured the appointments of leading members of MECCA, the Save Lake

Superior Association and the Northern Environmental Council as deputy director of the agency, director of the agency's Duluth field office, and member of the agency's governing citizen board.

Merritt was encouraged, on entering Dominick's room, even before Dominick opened his mouth. He saw that Dominick had with him a typescript version of the Ralph Nader report *Water Wasteland*. Merritt had urged Nader to look into the Reserve Mining controversy two years earlier and had worked with members of Nader's staff since then. He knew that the report contained a long chapter on Reserve that said everything he had hoped for. The chapter even documented from internal company papers Reserve's hurried attempt to cover its tailings delta with grass just before Secretary Udall's proposed visit in 1967 — the incident that had originally aroused Merritt's anger against Reserve. Together Merritt and Dominick had "rather elaborate discussions" about what Dominick intended to do.

The April 1971 session of the Lake Superior Enforcement Conference began with a report from the technical committee appointed by Murray Stein to consider on-land disposal and the deep pipe. Donald Mount had attended the technical committee's meetings as an adviser. He recalls that the demands of Governors Anderson and Lucey for on-land disposal put the technical committee in a political strait jacket. He personally felt that some form of continued in-lake disposal would not necessarily be more harmful to the environment than on-land disposal. At the last meeting of the technical committee, Mount had voiced his reservations to Grant Merritt with uncharacteristic bitterness. Looking back, Mount explains, "The prevailing feeling was that it's wrong to use water as a waste assimilation medium. So people focussed on water pollution to the exclusion of the problems created by land systems. I wasn't convinced that we'd ever get any kind of reasonable disposal conditions on land — and tailings impoundments can be pretty messy. I also got some estimates on the enormous amount of coal Reserve would have to burn to push 67,000 tons of tailings up over the ridge line behind Silver Bay every day. This was before the energy crisis, so I was mainly concerned that more land somewhere would be devastated to strip-mine the coal and the air would be polluted by burning it."

The technical committee achieved a unanimous report by putting aside Mount's reservations, to be dealt with another day. The report noted that the Northern Environmental Council, MECCA, and the Save Lake Superior Association had proposed that Reserve dispose of its tailings on land near Silver Bay at Lax Lake, just as Stoddard's report had proposed more than two years before. The only official reservations about the Lax Lake proposal which the report mentioned were those of the Minnesota Department of Natural Resources (the successor to the old State Department of Conservation). "While not making a judgment on the alternative," the Department suggested that Reserve relocate more than half of its plant — the crushing and separating operations — all the way back at its mine near Babbitt. The report flatly labelled Reserve's deep pipe proposal, as presented, "unacceptable" because it would not eliminate green water, it would not materially reduce the discharge of dissolved solids or suspended solids, and it would require the discharge of a chemical flocculant that "would have unknown ecological impact." The only concession to Mount in the technical committee's report was a recommendation that the enforcement conference "provide guidance to the discharger" in the form of criteria spelling out just what sort of disposal system would be acceptable to the State and Federal governments.

Reserve Mining Company had no back-up plan if the deep pipe was rejected. William DeLancey, the president of Republic Steel, later testified that the executives of Republic, Armco and Reserve met in March 1971 and decided to fight to stay in Lake Superior. C. William Verity, the chairman of Armco's board, explains: "if you are not willing to fight for your convictions when you have the facts available to you, and some of your opponents are acting emotionally, then I think it would be totally un-American to lie down and play dead." Edward Fride, Reserve's lawyer, and Kenneth Haley, the company's vice president for research and development, took part in the decision to fight to keep dumping tailings in Lake Superior. On April 22, Fride supported that decision by reiterating to the enforcement confer-ence what Reserve had told the technical committee. Reserve was unable to move its concentrating and separating operations to

Babbitt now for the same reasons they had been unable to build there in 1947: lack of sufficient water and suitable land. And Haley testified that any on-land tailings impoundment built near Silver Bay "would involve a huge system of dams and dikes, one of the largest in the world, and would represent a constant threat of leaks and rupture." In any event, after Reserve ceased operations, "surface waters would continue to erode any on-land tailings deposit until it would finally be washed into Lake Superior." Such an impoundment would destroy several square miles of "prime recreation country." And an impoundment would "present a very serious blowing dust problem . . . a nuisance to residents and tourists of the North Shore area."

David Dominick had seen enough. He thought to himself, he recalls: "Symbolically, this was the most important case in the country. Here was the last of the unpolluted Great Lakes; you could drink from it, see a hundred feet into it. And camped incongruously on its shore was a huge symbol of our industrial might run from the board rooms of two steel companies in Ohio. These companies were displaying themselves to be intransigent, stubborn . . . . I was generally frustrated that these guys could delay and delay and delay, forcing the government through tremendously expensive administrative proceedings. I thought that these must really be stubborn SOB's who were looking at their investment in this plant and their profits from it — the public interest and their image be damned. They were still living in the 19th century." On April 23, Dominick announced that he was recommending to Administrator Ruckelshaus that the Federal government abandon the Lake Superior Enforcement Conference and proceed directly against Reserve under an unused section of the Federal Water Pollution Control Act. Under this provision, the Administrator would notify Reserve that they were violating Federally-approved water quality standards and had 180 days to propose an acceptable plan for pollution abatement. If Reserve did not propose an acceptable plan, the Administrator could ask the Department of Justice to sue the company in Federal court. During this 180-day period, Dominick announced, EPA would "employ an independent consulting firm of national reputation to assist us in reaching an objective evaluation of the many technical, economic and environmental issues involved."

Grant Merritt quickly moved that the conference adopt Dominick's recommendation. First, Wisconsin's representative (expressing regret at the suddenness of Dominick's action), then Michigan's representative, voted to adopt Merritt's motion. In effect, the Federal-State enforcement conference declared bankruptcy and called in a receiver. As a final piece of business, Merritt made another motion, one he hadn't discussed with Dominick. He asked that the conference adopt a recommendation requiring Reserve to dispose of its tailings on land. After some sparring, Dominick agreed to make this recommendation unanimous, too. Merritt was happy to have the Federal government on record in favor of on-land disposal for the first time, despite the reservations Mount had expressed to the technical committee. Merritt thought that he hadn't exactly fooled Dominick, but he had persuaded him to adopt a position he hadn't thought through.

David Dominick recalls that he had talked with Ruckelshaus in Washington beforehand about his recommendation that the Administrator issue a 180-day notice to Reserve. But Ruckelshaus says that he was surprised at Dominick's recommendation. John Quarles says that he learned of Dominick's recommendation by watching the evening news. Publicly committed to a tough enforcement policy, Ruckelshaus and Quarles had no effective alternative to accepting Dominick's recommendation. They had allowed Dominick to go to Duluth as chairman of the enforcement conference and, Ruckelshaus says, "it was to some degree a question of not backing up the man in charge." On April 28, Ruckelshaus issued a 180-day notice to Reserve.

IV

The Shining Big-Sea-Water

Generations of visitors have sung the praises of Lake Superior. A decade before the American Revolution, Captain Jonathan Carver of Massachusetts crossed the lake and explored as far as the present site of Minneapolis-St. Paul, on a government expedition to discover a Northwest Passage. The Crown never paid Captain Carver the expenses of his expedition. Reduced to dire poverty, he published his *Travels* in an attempt to make up his loss. He didn't make money, but he left a glowing description of Lake Superior:

> When it was calm, and the sun shone bright, I could sit in my canoe, where the depth was upwards of six fathoms, and plainly see huge piles of stone at the bottom, of different shapes, some of which appeared as if they were hewn. The water at this time was as pure and transparent as air; and my canoe seemed as if it hung suspended in that element. It was impossible to look attentively through this limpid medium at the rocks below, without finding, before many minutes were elapsed, your head swim, and your eye no longer able to behold the dazzling scene.

(Carver's descendants gained posthumous revenge for the government's shabby treatment of the captain. They sold land claims on the basis of a spurious grant to Carver from the Sioux of several hundred square miles, including downtown St. Paul. As recently as the 1920's it was said, "If the present governor of Minnesota has not been addressed by some person believing himself a

rightful beneficiary of the claim, his experience is exceptional.")
In the early 19th century, George Heriot, a long-time civil servant
in the British government of Canada and an accomplished amateur
water colorist, wrote of Lake Superior in his *Travels*:

> The waters are more pure and pellucid than those of
> any other lake upon this globe, and the fish, as well as
> the rocks can be distinctly seen at a depth incredible to
> persons who have never visited those regions.

After the First World War, Webb Waldron, a free-lance jour-
nalist, visited Duluth to gather material for his *We Explore the
Great Lakes*. He interviewed "an old prospector and miner of
Duluth" — Grant Merritt's grandfather, Alfred — for background
before travelling up the Minnesota shore of Lake Superior to Isle
Royale. He wrote of his journey:

> The day was dazzling. The islands stood up, sharp,
> vivid, green, from a sea as vividly blue and so trans-
> parent that the bottom a hundred feet down seemed
> within reach of an oar.

But Lake Superior is best known to the world through the words
of a man who never saw it. When Henry Wadsworth Longfellow
wrote *The Song of Hiawatha*, he relied on the accounts of the
great surveyor Henry Schoolcraft, to describe the lake:

> Forth upon the Gitche Gumee,
> On the shining Big-Sea-Water...
> In his birch canoe exulting
> All alone went Hiawatha.
> Through the clear, transparent water
> He could see the fishes swimming
> Far down in the depths below him.

·   ·   ·

One fall evening in 1967 Mrs. Verna Mize was rhapsodizing
about her recent visit to Lake Superior in the same lyrical terms

that the lake has evoked for more than two hundred years. Mrs. Mize had been born in Michigan's Upper Penninsula. She recalls first falling in love with Lake Superior when she was taken to its shores at the age of 4. She had moved to suburban Washington, D.C., in the 30's, to become a career government secretary. But she and her husband continued to vacation often on Lake Superior, where she would spend hours walking along the shore. Now, on this fall evening, Mrs. Mize recalled her summer's vacation on the lake, telling a Washington friend how she had drunk from a cup dipped in its clear water. She became alarmed when her friend told her that thousands of tons of industrial waste were being dumped into the lake every day at Silver Bay, Minnesota. At 9:00 the next morning, she called Al Eisele, the Washington correspondent of the *Duluth News-Tribune,* who sent her an article describing the operations of Reserve Mining Company. The article increased her fear for the lake she loved.

Verna Mize's past political activities had never gone beyond modest efforts at civic improvement. She now wrote some letters to Congressmen about Reserve Mining Company. "I was really and truly idealistic," she says. "I thought that as soon as people on Capitol Hill knew, something would be done." Years went by and nothing was done. Mrs. Mize tried harder. She got sample bottles containing a milky gray suspension of tailings in water from the Save Lake Superior Association and began leaving the bottles on the desks of Great Lakes Congressmen and other public officials. "I began to learn," she says, "that I had to figure out how this case would affect each person I talked to." She also took her story to the press. Saul Friedman, a Washington correspondent for the *Detroit Free Press*, has written:

> Verna Mize came to see me on a cold, rainy Saturday
> when she would have been better off in her comfort-
> able home in one of Washington's suburbs. Like some-
> one appealing on behalf of a loved one, she asked . . .
> in her half-pleading half-nagging Midwestern twang:
> "Won't you help me save Lake Superior."

Mrs. Mize moved her typewriter next to her stove so that she could watch dinner while she composed "battle reports" to a steadily growing list of concerned citizens and friendly journalists across the country, conveying information about Reserve gathered from newspaper and magazine articles, telephone conversations with friendly low-level bureaucrats, and the replies of public officials to her letters. One of the people she wrote to was Grant Merritt, the Executive Director of the Minnesota Pollution Control Agency. Merritt began calling her regularly. "In effect," he says, "Verna became the Agency's Washington lobbyist on Reserve."

Before her 1970 vacation in the Upper Peninsula of Michigan, Mrs. Mize drafted a petition asking President Nixon's "speedy intervention to rescue Lake Superior from the ravages" of Reserve Mining Company. "Please, Mr. President," the petition said, "save 'the clear transparent water . . . the shining Big Sea water' for us and for posterity." She started with enough copies to get 300 signatures on the petition; at the end of two weeks she had gathered more than 5,000. She first took her petition to Murray Stein. "He was very rude," she recalls. She went to Russell Train, who had moved from the Department of the Interior to the Executive Office of the President, where he was chairman of the newly-created Council on Environmental Quality. She recalls Train putting her off by asking, "Have you talked to Congressman Blatnik about this?" She finally transmitted her petition to President Nixon through friends she had cultivated on the staffs of Michigan's U.S. Senators Philip Hart and Robert Griffin.

In the spring of 1971, Verna Mize was lobbying hard against Reserve. EPA Administrator William Ruckelshaus had already issued a 180-day notice to Reserve to abate its pollution, but the notice left important questions unanswered. Would EPA require Reserve to dispose of its tailings on land? If Reserve failed to meet EPA's requirements, would the agency go to court? Verna Mize worked to get Congressmen on record for a lawsuit unless Reserve agreed to on-land disposal. Grant Merritt and Governor Wendell Anderson of Minnesota cornered William Ruckelshaus in the back seat of a car to protest that the official summary of the last session of the Lake Superior Enforcement Conference omitted the conferees' unanimous recommendation that Reserve be required to dispose of its tailings on land. Ruckelshaus said that John Quarles, his Assistant Administrator for Enforcement, would make the necessary changes. Merritt showed Quarles the point in the transcript of the conference where David Dominick had agreed with this recommendation. Merritt recalls that Quarles' single-word comment was "Shithead." But Quarles made the changes.

In the summer and fall of 1971, Reserve, Armco and Republic intensified *their* lobbying efforts. C. William Verity, the Chairman of the Board of Armco Steel, supervised the preparation of a program — complete with three-dimensional model and visual aids — that explained Reserve Mining Company's existing operation and the deep pipe proposal. At private meetings arranged by Congressman Blatnik, senior executives of Armco and Republic, accompanied by Reserve's lawyer Edward Fride, presented this program to Senators and Senatorial staff members from Minnesota, Michigan and Ohio. Reserve retained former Secretary of Defense Clark Clifford as a consultant to deal with his former subordinates in the Army Corps of Engineers. Clifford introduced William DeLancey, the President of Republic Steel, to Edmund Muskie, chairman of the Senate's pollution control sub-committee and the front-runner for the Democratic Presidential nomination, for a similar presentation. The Armco and Republic executives also met with Russell Train of the President's Council on Environmental Quality and John Whitaker, a long-time Nixon aide. They tried to meet with William Ruckelshaus, but met instead with his Deputy Administrator, Robert Fri. "If Ruckelshaus knew he'd be involved in a major decision," Fri explains, "he'd throw any company request for a private meeting to me or John Quarles. I was probably tagged for this meeting, because I wasn't involved in the decision-making process." Quarles, who did have some responsibility for deciding what to do about Reserve, also heard the Armco and Republic presentation, but only inadvertently, he says. Congressman Blatnik invited Quarles to meet him on Capitol Hill. When Quarles arrived he found C. William Verity and William DeLancey there with their three-dimensional model and visual aids.

During 1971, Reserve Mining Company spent approximately $350,000 on lawyers and consultants to defend itself. And

Reserve returned approximately $19,000,000 in after-tax profits to Armco and Republic Steel.

None of the people in Washington who heard the presentation of Reserve, Armco and Republic seemed to have a clear idea of what the companies expected them to do. One of them dismissed the presentation as "a dog-and-pony show." And citizen opposition to the companies stiffened when Saul Friedman and Al Eisele wrote detailed stories on their lobbying effort under bold headlines: "LOBBYISTS SWARM ON CAPITOL TO HEAD OFF POLLUTION ORDER," "POLLUTER OF LAKE SEEKS WHITE HOUSE RELIEF," "RESERVE MINING CASE A CLASSIC OF POLLUTION POLITICS." "We thought that maybe we had done ourselves a service," says C. William Verity. "Well, we later realized that that hadn't been the right approach. We didn't influence anybody." Verna Mize had been quietly at work for months in many of the offices where the companies made their presentation. And the offices she hadn't visited before, she visited now. Russell Train and John Whitaker yielded to her demands that they grant a meeting to her, accompanied by Charles Stoddard for technical support. She doubts her interview had much effect. "The companies had made a professional presentation," she says. "All I could do was pour my heart out." She arranged to have Grant Merritt meet Senator Robert Griffin of Michigan in order to put Republican pressure on William Ruckelshaus to request a suit against Reserve. She insisted upon and won a personal meeting with Ruckelshaus. Ruckelshaus recalls that "Verna Mize was a constant and imaginative lobbyist for strong action against Reserve — she even wrote to my wife for help." By October, Merritt recalls, Mrs. Mize had lined up the senators of Michigan, Illinois and Indiana to write Ruckelshaus in favor of filing suit. Wisconsin's senators deferred to Minnesota's. Senator Walter Mondale of Minnesota (whom Merritt visited regularly) met in his office with William Ruckelshaus to tell him, "You do what you have to do, and we'll support you."

EPA's 180-day notice to Reserve expired on October 25, 1971. The job of preparing the agency's next step then fell to John Quarles' new director of litigation, Thomas H. Truitt. Truitt projected self-confidence as much as Quarles projected caution. A trial lawyer and former lobbyist for the pesticides industry, he had tousled blond hair, blue eyes and a frequent wide smile above his ever-present bow-tie. The bright but inexperienced young lawyers on his staff were, like him, liberal Democrats, eager to be where the action was. Truitt put them to work combing the agency's files and preparing an action memorandum. In December 1971, Truitt reported to Quarles and Ruckelshaus that the agency's evidence for any court case against Reserve was "thin." To obtain a court order halting Reserve's discharge, the agency would have to prove that Reserve was more probably than not causing irreparable injury to Lake Superior. The government would have a difficult time constructing a winning case largely on the basis of a handful of laboratory experiments. There were probably many cases where the agency had much stronger evidence of pollution; the government should go to court on those cases first. Furthermore, Truitt noted, the government's problems in court against Reserve would not be limited to proving irreparable harm from the company's present method of tailings disposal. The independent consulting firm hired by David Dominick to study alternative means of disposal was composed of sanitary engineers without experience in the mining business, and their work — performed at a cost to the agency of more than $100,000 — was "a virtual nullity." However, Truitt told Ruckelshaus that if he still wanted to ask the Department of Justice to sue Reserve, the agency should jump into the case with both feet. It should ask the Department to sue Reserve for violating every conceivable statute. And it should ask the Department to name Reserve's parent companies, Armco Steel and Republic Steel, as defendants in the suit to make clear that the agency meant business. This would also make it easier for the trial court to find out just how much the companies could afford for pollution control.

Truitt later testified with wry understatement that his proposal to request suit against Armco and Republic was "a matter of some sensitivity" within the Administration, since both corporations had powerful friends in the White House. The Department of Justice had only recently filed a series of lawsuits against polluting industries under an obscure act of Congress which had lain dormant for 60 years until it had been reinterpreted in a

surprising opinion delivered for the Supreme Court by Justice
William O. Douglas. A senior career lawyer at the Natural
Resources Division of the Department of Justice, Walter Kiechel,
explains: "We developed two criteria for filing any suit under this
act. Is the discharger recalcitrant in meeting abatement schedules
set by enforcement conferences? Is the discharge dangerous? Most
of the steel companies qualified." The Department had routinely
filed suits against Republic Steel for its discharges into the
Cuyahoga River in Ohio and against Armco Steel for its
discharges into the Houston Ship Channel in Texas. The *Armco*
case came to trial in the summer of 1971. At the end of the trial,
U.S. District Judge Allen B. Hannay ordered Armco to cease
immediately its discharge of a variety of toxic substances,
including 975 pounds a day of cyanide, into the Houston Ship
Channel. Ten days later, C. William Verity, the Chairman of the
Board of Armco Steel and Vice Chairman of the Republican
Finance Committee in Ohio, wrote to President Nixon, protesting
that the judge's order had "shut down a major part of our
operation" in Houston and "eliminated about 300 jobs in one
stroke of the pen." Verity sent a copy of his letter to Presidential
Counsellor Peter Flanigan. Flanigan summoned John Quarles to
his White House office and Flanigan's office called the politically-
appointed Assistant Attorney General for Natural Resources, to
tell them to get Judge Hannay's order lifted and negotiate a
substitute decree satisfactory to Armco. Flanigan's instructions
were passed down the line. Walter Kiechel of the Natural
Resources Division later testified, "I was dismayed." Thomas
Truitt and other EPA lawyers protested Flanigan's intervention
directly to William Ruckelshaus, and President Nixon's
environmental aide John Whitaker (a frequent ally of
Ruckelshaus) stepped in to counteract Flanigan. Lawyers for the
Justice Department and for EPA (led by Truitt) ultimately were
able to negotiate a substitute decree with Armco, which achieved
most of the government's original objectives in filing suit. There
the matter would have rested, had not the Assistant Attorney
General for Natural Resources appeared before a Congressional
committee to deny rumors of White House interference; his denial
was supported by the evasive testimony of John Quarles. When

the same Congressional committee subsequently discovered a government memorandum documenting the interference, Quarles and the Assistant Attorney General were grilled at a well-publicized hearing. By the end of 1971, Armco Steel was regarded in and out of government as a prime example of backstairs political manipulation and influence-peddling to escape the law.

On January 20, 1972, William Ruckelshaus sent a public letter to the Department of Justice asking them to sue Reserve Mining Company. His letter did not mention Armco Steel or Republic Steel. A story circulated within EPA at the time that Ruckelshaus had refused to request suit against the parent corporations, unless he could get prior clearance from Attorney General Mitchell (who was even then secretly acting as the President's campaign manager). Five years after the event, none of the people who took part in the decision to send the letter had a clear enough recollection to confirm or deny this story. However, the vehemence with which attorneys for the companies objected to any legal inquiries into the non-joinder of Armco and Republic has left a number of observers with the suspicion that the companies have something to hide.

Ruckelshaus' letter did not ask the Department of Justice to seek an order requiring on-land disposal, only one "abating Reserve's pollution of Lake Superior." This ducked the question of whether the deep pipe was a satisfactory plan to abate that pollution. Despite David Dominick's concurrence in recommending on-land disposal at the Lake Superior Enforcement Conference, the lawyers in EPA's enforcement office, from Truitt's staff on up, doubted the agency could prove a case for on-land disposal with the existing evidence — particularly in light of the failure of the agency's engineering study. At the same time he wrote the Department of Justice, Ruckelshaus asked the governors of Minnesota, Wisconsin and Michigan to join in the suit. But he personally warned Governor Anderson and Governor Lucey, "It ain't going to be as easy as you think."

The EPA enforcement staff may have been less than enthusiastic about requesting suit against Reserve Mining Company, but, Ruckelshaus recalls, "I had to take into account more than just scientific principles of what were the most serious pollution problems. EPA had to be perceived as capable of resolving this kind of issue . . . . I thought, this is just going on and on, and I didn't see any alternatives from the staff that looked like they would resolve it. There were people running against this company in three States. The whole issue had become so politicized that the States just weren't interested in negotiating a solution. We had to get all the parties together under one umbrella, subject to the same court. So we could either institute legal process or wait to be sued" — by Reserve, by the States, by the environmentalists, or by all of them.

One evening while Ruckelshaus and the EPA staff were drafting his letter to the Department of Justice, Richard Fairbanks, a young assistant to Presidential aide John Whitaker, was visited in his White House office by Reserve's lawyer, Edward Fride. After this visit, Fairbanks wrote a memo to Presidential Counsellor John Ehrlichman, asking that he approve Ruckelshaus' sending of the letter. The memo noted that there was tremendous popular opposition to Reserve's discharge. ("We must have had 20,000 letters on Reserve," Fairbanks says.) If Ruckelshaus did not request a lawsuit, the memo explained, it would be seen as a sell-out to a big political contributor. Since Ruckelshaus' letter only sought an order "abating Reserve's pollution," not requiring on-land disposal, the letter did not knuckle under to the environmental "lunatic fringe" — it simply got the problem out of the executive department and into court "in a neutral way." (Fairbanks explains with a rueful smile that the somewhat cynical tone of his memo was necessary to White House paperwork at the time.) Ruckelshaus recalls that when he visited John Ehrlichman to get final clearance for his letter, Ehrlichman's reaction was "What are you bringing this to me for? Why not go ahead and file?" There was not much substance to published speculation that the White House staff was pushing him around, Ruckelshaus says. Maurice Stans, the Secretary of Commerce and the President's once and future campaign finance chairman, did "raise hell . . . but then he didn't think we should sue *anybody*." Stans took his advice on environmental matters from a group which he created, the National Industrial Pollution Control Council. According to one of its members, C. William Verity of Armco

Steel, the Council was "made up of people who were involved in businesses that undoubtedly had a pollution problem."

On February 17, 1972, the Department of Justice filed a formal complaint captioned *United States of America* v. *Reserve Mining Company* with the United States District Court for the District of Minnesota in Minneapolis. The prayer of the complaint — that the court order Reserve "to abate the pollution from the discharge of taconite ore waste into Lake Superior" — reflected the ambiguity of Ruckelshaus' letter and Fairbanks' White House memo. Armco and Republic Steel were not named as defendants. John Quarles told EPA colleagues that he was caught in a rush hour traffic jam about this time, when he saw the limousine of John Mitchell's successor, Richard Kleindeinst. Quarles rolled down his window and thanked Kleindeinst for filing suit. Kleindeinst laughed and said, "That's all right. We'll settle after the election."

On April 10, 1972, the Honorable Miles W. Lord, United States District Judge for the District of Minnesota, held his first pretrial hearing in the *Reserve Mining* case. By this time, the United States had been joined as plaintiff in the case by four environmental groups, including the Northern Environmental Council and the Save Lake Superior Association, and by the States of Michigan and Wisconsin. (For procedural reasons, the State of Minnesota did not join until some months later.) Reserve had been joined as defendant by six local governments and five groups such as the Duluth Area Chamber of Commerce and the Northeastern Minnesota Development Association. The counsel tables in Judge Lord's courtroom were crowded for this hearing with lawyers watchful as horse players at the paddock, eager to "dope out" the judge's performance. The judge's attitude was especially important in this case; since it was a suit for an injunction, he would be sitting as a court of equity, without a jury. He would determine all disputed legal and factual issues himself.

Judge Lord had spent 20 years in Minnesota politics and his personal history was well known. He was born and grew up near the Mesabi Iron Range town of Crosby. He worked his way through college and the University of Minnesota Law School as a janitor, logger, restaurant operator, ditch digger, postal clerk and bellhop. An accomplished raconteur, the judge often tells how he boxed as a Golden Gloves middleweight in his youth and how he was knocked down 17 times in the three rounds of one championship fight. His pugnacity and stamina combined with a quick mind and folksy sense of humor to make him a formidable politician: he was elected State Attorney General on the Democratic-Farmer-Labor ticket in 1954 and reelected in 1956 and 1958. These same qualities didn't always serve him so well in the courtroom. Shortly before he retired as attorney general, Lord became involved in a bitter dispute with the conservative Chief Justice of the State Supreme Court. The legislature had adopted two conflicting laws on daylight saving time within one week of each other. The commissioners of three metropolitan counties adopted daylight saving time under a local option clause of the first law, and a theater owner petitioned the Supreme Court for relief under the second law. The day before the time change was to take effect the Chief Justice signed a writ prohibiting the commissioners from imposing daylight saving time. Attorney General Lord went on radio and TV that night to say that the counties' daylight saving time resolutions were valid under the first law and that the Chief Justice's writ only applied to future actions in any event. The angry justices of the Supreme Court ordered the attorney general to appear for a hearing on his "professional conduct." Lord then obtained a letter from the State's DFL governor advising him not to appear on the grounds of "separation of powers." The Supreme Court "severely censured" Attorney General Lord, *in absentia,* stating that his radio and TV appearances misled the public "to believe that this court had done something improper and to the detriment of the public, while he, as attorney general, was carrying on the battle against the court for the benefit of the public." His appearances had been motivated, the court suggested, "by an inordinate desire for publicity or by a desire to gain political popularity by undermining confidence in the integrity and impartiality of our judicial system." His run-in with the Chief Justice, Judge Lord conceded to reporters a few years later, had been "long on personalities and short on legal arguments" and it had hurt his credibility. But his career rebounded when President Kennedy appointed him United States District Attorney for Minnesota. Lord told a reporter that he was sounded out for an important job in the Department of Justice about that time; he said he'd be interested if they'd move the office building from Washington to suburban Minneapolis. His participation in national politics never really extended beyond his support for the Presidential aspirations of his old friend and companion from the campaign trail, Hubert Humphrey. With Vice President Humphrey's support, President Johnson appointed Lord, at age 46, to the Federal bench. Judge Lord made no secret of his continuing interest in Minnesota politics. His youngest son wasn't out of law school in 1972, but was already a rising star in the DFL, with his father's help.

At the opening of the April 10 hearing, Judge Lord said that he had "some feelers out" to see if a judge from another State would come in and hear the case. His own family were iron miners, who had been hit hard by the Depression; they hadn't thought anything, the Judge said, of filling a lake near Crosby with tailings. In 1964, he and Hubert Humphrey and their wives had been vacation guests of Reserve's Edward Schmid at Silver Bay. "I was not an early supporter of that Taconite Amendment," he explained. "However, I believe on that trip, I was convinced . . . . " For this case, Reserve had hired as co-counsel to Edward Fride, Robert J. Sheran, a DFL colleague of the judge, who had just resigned after seven years as a State Supreme Court Justice. Judge Lord greeted Sheran, a polite, dignified man with wavy gray hair and a polished oratorical style, as "my friend, Bob Sheran here, whom I greatly respect and admire." During the hearing, the judge reassured counsel for the local governments about Reserve: "They are not going to be forced to close their operation. I don't think anything that I will do here will cost them one job . . . . When the labor union leaders came to me and suggested that this proceeding might put them out of jobs, I said I didn't think it was possible under the law to do that." Judge Lord also asked rhetorically, "Did somebody tell me when they brought the case, they announced they were bringing a weak case?" After sorting out a complicated tangle of motions and counter-motions, he concluded "I have heard enough to know that I am not going to get any other out-of-state judge to come into this case." Edward Fride replied for Reserve, "I am pleased to hear that, your honor."

Sitting in the courtroom, Thomas Truitt of EPA was not at all pleased. He was disturbed by Judge Lord's remarks. He worried that the judge was "too closely allied with the Democratic-Farmer-Labor Party" which had encouraged Reserve over the years, and "overly sensitive to employment and economic impacts," as balanced against protection of the environment. Truitt huddled with Department of Justice lawyers to discuss filing a motion that the judge disqualify himself. They finally decided that Judge Lord was as good as they were likely to get, and dropped the idea of the motion.

While Judge Lord waded through procedural complexities during 1972, Truitt's staff worried about how to strengthen the government's case against Reserve. In *Cleaning Up America* John Quarles has written of EPA's early pollution abatement cases with detachment:

> There was one curious feature of the early EPA enforcement program: almost the entire emphasis was placed on beginning the actions . . . . The difficulties of pursuing an action through to completion — achieving an actual clean up program — seemed scarcely to be noticed, especially at first . . . . In most cases . . . the hopes raised by bringing suit against the polluter were destined never to be fulfilled.

Quarles' use of the passive voice conceals that he was EPA's Assistant Administrator for Enforcement — the man finally responsible for misplacing emphasis, for not noticing difficulties, for raising false hopes. Truitt's young staff lawyers realized that any push to strengthen the government's case against Reserve would not come from their superiors, but from themselves. One of the lawyers, Michael Gross, says "All the bureaucrats were pooh-poohing this case as unwinnable. When I first saw Lake Superior, it was imposing — something special. I thought the government had an interest in protecting it. Winning the case was a challenge to me as an individual."

In the early months of 1972, the lawyers met a number of times with Donald Mount, the Director of EPA's National Water Quality Laboratory in Duluth. The government would be hard pressed to make a convincing case against Reserve unless Mount was willing to commit his scientific prestige and the resources of his laboratory to the effort. For the moment, Mount confined himself to pointing out at great length the weaknesses in the government's case; he was making no commitments. The lawyers' description of Mount at this time matches Mount's description of Carl Klein two years before: "He seemed to just want the problem to go away." Mount and his family had come to enjoy Duluth and the farm he'd bought outside of town. He was on his way to becoming EPA's longest-tenured lab director. "By 1972," Mount says, "I was tired of the constant parade of people from Washington trying to deal with Reserve, of their indecision, their lack of any position, and their failure to fund a penny's worth of research." He was tired of murmured comments in supermarkets and anonymous phone calls in the night; people said that he was harassing Reserve or, on the other hand, that he was "Blatnik's stooge." And he was tired of prodding, accusing letters from Verna Mize to himself and his superiors. Mount now had a large pane of one-way glass in his office door. Visitors who talked to him about Reserve commonly described him as "enigmatic." "Federal scientists like Mount have everything to lose and nothing to gain from getting involved in controversies where strong economic interests are at stake," says Charles Stoddard. "They just don't have access to any agency support for positions on controversial issues."

In the spring of 1972, almost by accident, Michael Gross met Gary Glass. Glass was as encouraging as Mount had been discouraging. Glass and Mount were increasingly at odds in the laboratory. In 1970 and 1971, Glass had asked Mount to authorize major studies more directly related to immediate social concerns than the lab's standard aquatic bioassays — one study of carcinogens in water supplies and another of organic contaminants in fish. These studies would have given Glass control of a large part of the laboratory's manpower and equipment. Mount had turned both studies down. Now Glass saw an opportunity to bypass

Mount and get the laboratory "to do a large, coordinated study, according to *my* specifications." Glass said he'd undertake the design of an evidence-gathering program on several conditions: EPA headquarters would have to find someone else for the time-consuming job of giving scientific advice to the government's lawyers; headquarters would have to require the completion of a comprehensive program, not a piecemeal one as in the past; and the agency would have to look seriously at the best environmental alternative to in-lake disposal. (Glass had talked to people who had examined Reserve's finances. They thought the company could afford to move its crushing and separating operations back to its mine at Babbitt and dispose of its tailings there, as the Minnesota Department of Natural Resources had suggested the previous year. This would eliminate many problems that would result from a tailings impoundment near the shore of Lake Superior. It would remove the tailings from the Lake Superior drainage basin permanently, it would eliminate blowing dust in the town of Silver Bay, and it would decrease, rather than increase, energy consumption.) Michael Gross returned to Washington with word of his discovery. There were long discussions with Thomas Truitt, who was worried that his staff might so antagonize Mount as to cost Glass his job. He finally decided to go ahead with Glass' research program.

Truitt saw clearly that he'd never get Glass' research program approved without the support of John Quarles' senior scientific advisor, Dr. A. Gordon Everett. A petroleum geologist and former deputy to Carl Klein, Everett saw his job as providing Quarles with a check on the quality of scientific work done in the field and with interdisciplinary scientific advice integrating the treatment of air, water, and economic problems. In sum, Everett says, his office was an attempt to overcome a common phenomenon of government, that "officials above the level of GS-13 or GS-14 [the pay grade of a postmaster in a city of medium size] don't understand the substance of the decisions they're asked to make." Former members of Everett's staff praise him as a questioning scientist who respected differences of opinion. Nevertheless, Truitt's staff lawyers were reluctant to deal with Everett. He was, Truitt recalls, "very turf conscious." One of Everett's leading patrons in the bureaucracy muses that Everett's scientific advice usually seemed aimed, partly at least, to assure he "had a good, strong role." Everett's involvement in scientific programs almost always entailed distracting hassles over control, and he seemed addicted to big, time-consuming meetings that Truitt dismissed contemptuously as "elephant fucks." (Truitt explains, "An elephant fuck is a large, boring, ridiculous meeting — enormous awkward animals making a lot of noise, and perhaps a baby elephant will follow in a couple of years.") Truitt's lawyers were also suspicious that Everett's staff, top-heavy with geologists, had given them unsound ecological advice in the past.

Truitt, an engaging talker who could switch effortlessly from gross flattery to disarming candor and back, met Everett and told him he wanted to pursue the program outlined by Glass. "Gordon," Truitt said, "we'd rather have you in the tub pissing out, than out of the tub pissing in." Everett agreed to look at Glass' research program. After his staff had massaged the program, Glass convinced them to restore it to its original shape. Glass' previous work on the case gave him great confidence in his research program. He chuckles, "It was like betting on a race you'd already seen." Truitt and Everett approached a reluctant John Quarles for money to fund Glass' program. Truitt recalls telling Quarles "John, the people who know most about this case are in this room, and they're all telling you you need to spend more money." Michael Gross also called a friend on the staff of U.S. Senator Philip Hart. The friend arranged a letter from the Senator to Ruckelshaus asking if EPA was now gathering the environmental and engineering evidence necessary to build a winning case against Reserve. Quarles was able to send Senator Hart an affirmative response after he agreed with Truitt to allocate $100,000 for studies in Lake Superior to be coordinated by Glass under Mount's direction and $50,000 for a study by a consulting engineering firm to be coordinated by Michael Gross.

In May 1972, Truitt found Donald Mount and called him out of a National Science Foundation meeting in Washington. Over a beer, Truitt told him headquarters was committing $100,000 to study the effects of Reserve's discharge in Lake Superior. President Nixon had just ordered the mining of North Vietnam's harbors and the two men joked grimly about whether the country would be blown away before the studies could be started. Mount says, "I was surprised. It was a turning point — the first evidence I had that Washington was serious about this case." But Mount continued to raise a troubling question. He asked Truitt: suppose this research program goes off without a hitch. Suppose the program proves the subtle effects Reserve's tailings are having on Lake Superior, and Reserve asks "So what?" On-land disposal near Silver Bay might harm the environment more than in-lake disposal. And on-land disposal near the company's mine at Babbitt might cost more than a hundred million dollars and disrupt the lives of a thousand workers. How could EPA justify seeking a court order that Reserve dispose of its tailings on land, faced with that "So what?" Truitt knew that EPA's hierarchy had not faced Mount's complex balancing question in the past and they were unlikely to do so in the future. He could only say not to worry, that Reserve was too locked-in to dumping in Lake Superior and to denying any possible effect, to raise his question publicly. In the meantime, Mount should stick to his new assignment: carrying out Glass' research program.

The machinery of the EPA bureaucracy creaked and clanked and groaned and slowly turned Glass' plan into action. The wheels were assiduously oiled by the working-level members of Gordon Everett's staff, who had a thorough knowledge of the bureaucratic apparatus. (Two of them regularly scavenged through key agency waste baskets at 6:30 a.m., looking for useful information.) Everett's office contacted dozens of agency scientists from coast to coast, lining up necessary manpower and equipment. They drafted a memo for Deputy Administrator Fri to send every division of the Agency asking that everyone assign "the highest priority" to Glass' program and concluding, "The Administrator and I consider it crucial that this case be won. I know you share our sentiments." The prettiest woman on Everett's staff volunteered to hand-carry the memo through the complicated chain of command, to assure that everyone up to and including Fri signed off. Glass chartered the *Telson Queen*, a privately-owned converted minesweeper, as a research vessel for the summer. During the remainder of 1972, government and academic scientists converged on Duluth — bacteriologists from Naragansett, Rhode Island, algalogists from Milwaukee, Wisconsin, oceanographers from Corvallis, Oregon.

Gary Glass worked obsessively to see that every sample in his program was taken and analyzed. Mount proposed cuts at various points on the grounds that there wasn't enough manpower or equipment or time. Glass told visitors from Washington of his dark suspicions that Mount would sabotage his program, if it threatened his precarious balancing act on Reserve. Mount told the same visitors that Glass' officious nit-picking was ruining the morale of his coworkers and unnecessarily delaying completion of Glass' own work. It did not help their strained relations that Everett or Truitt, or both, often intervened to referee disputes between Mount and his nominal subordinate. In mid-summer Glass ruptured a lumbar disc carrying water samples. For weeks he suffered excruciating pain running from his lower back down his legs, whenever his spinal column moved. Truitt authorized him to buy a special chair for his office, and he stayed on the job, tending to the unforeseen problems that bedevil a complicated program: just what was the precise legal description of Michigan's boundary in Lake Superior? Would he order the captain of the *Telson Queen* to keep his dog off deck while bacteriological samples were being taken? And so on. Glass' father died of gastrointestinal cancer at the beginning of October and Glass kept working. Mount says, "Gary was a stronger force driving the government to pursue the Reserve investigation than all the environmentalists."

Donald Mount regularly gathered the principal investigators for Glass' research program at his lab, much as Charles Stoddard had done four years before, keeping up with leads provided by ongoing work, enforcing deadlines, outlining tentative conclusions. He kept the most loquacious of his colleagues in check by turning over a small hour-glass egg-timer as each of them began to speak. These meetings kept pressure to produce results on Federal scientists, who are inclined as a group to be very cautious: "The general feeling seemed to be that you back off a couple of steps from what you can prove, in order to avoid any possibility of overstating your case," says one scientist who attended the meetings.

Gary Glass' 1972 research program amounted to an elaborate field test of the validity of the conclusions that Mount had written for Charles Stoddard's Taconite Study Group four years earlier. With pretrial maneuvering in the *Reserve Mining* case drawing slowly to a close, Mount took a few days to sit down and review the results of Glass' program:

(1) Glass calculated that every day Reserve discharged over one billion trillion tailings particles finer than 5 microns in diameter (smaller than the size of a red blood cell) — more than 100,000 such particles for every liter of water in the lake. Dr. James Kramer of Canada's McMaster University, a leading authority on the sedimentary geology of the Great Lakes, calculated that Reserve's rate of discharge of tailings was some 5 to 10 times greater than the total rate for all other sources of sedimentation in Lake Superior, man-made and natural, American and Canadian. Reserve was, he concluded, a major geological event in the history of the world's largest expanse of fresh water, comparable to the arrival of European civilization.

(2) New evidence confirmed that the spread of Reserve's tailings in Lake Superior could be traced by identifying cummingtonite-grunerite in samples. Reserve estimated that fully one-third of their fine tailings consisted of cummingtonite-grunerite. When the plant was closed for regularly-scheduled maintenance, the National Water Quality Laboratory found that concentrations of cummingtonite-grunerite 20 feet and 40 feet below the surface of Lake Superior southwest of Silver Bay, gradually declined below the limits of detection by x-ray diffraction — less than two parts per hundred million. The laboratory could not find cummingtonite-grunerite in repeated samplings of dozens of Lake Superior tributaries. Nevertheless, Reserve continued to claim that tributaries were a source of measurable amounts of cummingtonite-grunerite in the lake, making the mineral unreliable as a tracer of tailings. One evening, a scientist from the laboratory reviewed copies of Reserve's x-ray diffraction patterns with Dr. William Phinney, the former director of the Minnesota Geological Survey. As chief geologist for the manned spaceflight

program of the National Aeronautics and Space Administration, in charge of the collection and analysis of moon rocks, Phinney was now one of the most influential geologists in the world. The two men looked at the patterns for each tributary where Reserve claimed to have identified cummingtonite-grunerite. As they started through the patterns, Phinney looked concerned. "There must be a mistake here," he muttered. In pattern after pattern, he could not find any peaks recording the reflection of intense x-rays at angles characteristic of cummingtonite-grunerite; Reserve was claiming to find the mineral in the streams, not on the basis of characteristic peaks, but on the basis of "background hash" (small random squiggles made on the pattern by the recording pen). As Phinney worked on, he began smiling: "They've got to be kidding." By the end of the evening the two men were laughing over the patterns like two kids watching cartoons.

(3) Oceanographers sank weighted plastic discs, called bottom drifters, 900 feet into Lake Superior off Reserve's tailings delta. Several of the bottom drifters were recovered, all in the area of Duluth, one from the screen of the Duluth water intake. Extensive measurements using current meters, bathythermographs, transmissometers, nephelometers and radioactive tracers determined a number of mechanisms, in addition to bottom currents, which distributed fine tailings throughout much of Lake Superior. Scuba divers for Stoddard's taconite study group had photographed fine tailings peeling off the density current created by Reserve's discharge during the summer at the thermocline, 60 to 120 feet below the surface of the lake; the 1972 data suggested that a "winter thermocline" 300 to 500 feet deep might strip off even more of the tailings. Even when the density current carried fine tailings deep into the lake they could be kept suspended by vertical turbulence below the thermocline, by internal waves reaching as deep as 1,000 feet, by upwellings, and by turnovers when the thermoclines broke up in the spring and fall. The data were examined by Dr. Robert Dill of the National Oceanic and Atmospheric Administration, an oceanographic colleague of Jacques Cousteau, who had worked in all the world's major research submersibles. If Reserve were to quit dumping, Dill

estimated, it would be 2 to 3 months before there would be a 90% reduction in the amount of fine tailings at the Duluth water intake, 65 feet below the surface of Lake Superior; it would be 15 months before the lake would be clear of fine tailings down to the 600 foot depth.

(4) Tailings contributed to a 200-foot thick lens of turbid water deep in the lake which reduced water clarity by more than 25% over an area of 600 square miles. Two high-altitude aerial reconnaisance missions flown by the Air Force and by NASA photographed masses of cloudy green surface water extending southwest of Reserve's plant as far as Duluth. Arthur Dybdahl, an expert in optical physics from EPA's Denver Field Investigation Center, designed the photographic equipment for the RF-4C Phantoms of the Air Force and directed their overflight of Lake Superior; he called the green water discoloration unique in his experience of dozens of aerial reconnaisance surveys of water pollution around the country. Samples were taken from the surface of one of the green water masses and analyzed by x-ray diffraction; 90% of the suspended solids in the samples were tailings.

(5) Gary Glass devised a method to calculate the total amount of dissolved chemicals which Reserve added to Lake Superior. He had previously worked out one component of that total: by reviewing Reserve's own analyses of the dissolved chemicals in its intake and discharge water, he determined that the waste water discharged by the plant each day contained approximately 50,000 pounds of dissolved chemicals more than the intake water. This gave him the amount of dissolved chemicals added to Lake Superior water as it passed through the plant. Glass was now ready to calculate the second component of the total. From the results of his own laboratory experiments, he estimated the amount of chemicals that dissolved into Lake Superior from fine tailings *after* the tailings were discharged: this amount came to approximately 150,000 pounds a day. Donald Mount pointed out that Glass' laboratory results were confirmed by similar tests of solubility performed for Reserve by a graduate student under the direction of Professor G. Fred Lee. Glass now carried out an elegant study of core samples taken from the lake

bottom, refining the state of the art in environmental chemistry. He showed increased levels of dissolved chemicals in the bottom water between settled tailings particles covering 100 square miles of the lake floor (levels of dissolved copper in this bottom water were high enough to kill some aquatic organisms), and he also showed the gradual diffusion of dissolved chemicals from the bottom water to the main body of the lake. Since G. Fred Lee had brought into question the chemical analyses performed for Stoddard's Taconite Study Group, Glass' was the first conclusive field demonstration that Reserve's discharge had a measurable effect on the level of dissolved chemicals in Lake Superior.

(6) A team of scientists conducted exhaustive statistical tests of all of the samples of bottom-dwelling organisms which had been taken along the Minnesota shore of Lake Superior. They looked particularly at populations of tiny (less than an inch long) freshwater shrimp, a pollution-sensitive relict with a diminishing habitat in the glacial lakes of the northern hemisphere. Populations of the shrimp were reduced for at least 30-40 miles southwest of Reserve's plant according to the team, which was led by Professor E. B. Henson of the University of Vermont, a specialist in the life history of the creatures. Scientists from the National Water Quality Laboratory trawled along the Minnesota shore for sculpin, a relatively sedentary deep water fish that provides food for lake herring and trout. They found that the stomachs of sculpins contained fewer fresh water shrimp as they neared Reserve's discharge; it appeared that the sculpins were eating fish eggs to replace the shrimp. Donald Mount described this as the first evidence that changes caused by Reserve's tailings were passed up the food chain and had ecological significance.

(7) Other attempts to demonstrate the effects of Reserve's discharge on Lake Superior were less successful. No statistically significant differences could be found between metals contamination in the flesh of sculpins netted southwest of Reserve and those netted elsewhere in the lake; however, Mount wrote, metals from neutron-activated tailings suspended in water could be traced into the livers and kidneys of fish exposed to such tailings in more sensitive laboratory tests. The 1972 studies did not find any clear-cut increases in populations of Lake Superior

bacteria which cause human disease that could be attributed to tailings, but laboratory tests showed that the bacteria attached to tailings when they were discharged grew more than bacteria in lake water without tailings. (All of the National Water Quality Laboratory's tests on bacteria had been rerun after Glass discovered that their bacteriologist's claim to a Ph.D. was fraudulent.) Another study, Mount noted, "failed to show differences relatable to tailings" in the growth of algae attached to pieces of net suspended in the surface waters of Lake Superior; but laboratory tests demonstrating a stimulatory effect on attached algae revealed that the nets "may not have been left sufficiently long to show this stimulation."

(8) One of the largest industrial design firms in the country — the International Engineering Company, a San Francisco-based subsidiary of Morrison-Knudsen, the construction conglomerate — reported that Reserve Mining Company could rebuild its crushing and separating facilities (and dispose of its tailings) near its Babbitt mine at an estimated capital cost of $189 million. Because new facilities would enable Reserve to improve the quality of its iron pellets with a lower expenditure of energy, Reserve could, at the same time, actually *increase* its parent corporations' profit per ton of pellets slightly, from $1.90 to $2.15.

In his official report, Donald Mount summarized the results of Glass' research program:

> The 1972 studies have supplemented and increased confidence in the effects identified in earlier studies. The distribution and persistence of tailings in the Lake is greater than previously shown. Chemical, physical and biological effects have been demonstrated in the Lake, and tailings as the cause have been implicated by controlled laboratory tests. The changes measured in the Lake were difficult to demonstrate, partly because large changes are needed to be clearly measurable and fortunately changes do not appear to be that large, as yet.

Reserve still refused to acknowledge that its discharge had any effect on Lake Superior. But Mount's "So what?" still hung heavily over the government's preparations for the *Reserve Mining* trial at the end of 1972. How would the government use the results of this research to justify its request for a court order that Reserve cease dumping into Lake Superior?

. . .

Preparing for trial was the job of a lawyer at the Natural Resources Division of the Department of Justice in Washington, sitting behind a government-issue desk off a narrow twisting corridor, in an office barely big enough for a couple of chairs and a few khaki green filing cabinets. John P. Hills, 37, was short, conservatively dressed, with a smooth face behind large rimless glasses, his hair prematurely white. He had none of the commanding physical presence of more typical trial lawyers like Reserve's Edward Fride and Robert Sheran. When angered, Hills would sink into stony silence rather than rise to rhetorical flourishes. A casual observer might have dismissed Hills as an insignificant bureaucrat, not likely to be much of a threat in litigation, but he had a tough reputation among his colleagues in the Division as "something of a maverick, a good trial lawyer who didn't like to compromise."

Hills was the son of a Nantucket fisherman and yacht broker. He fished with his father almost as soon as he could walk and first sailed a boat alone at age 7. After law school, he moved to his wife's hometown, Memphis, Tennessee. Almost immediately, he landed on the front pages. Due to a falling out among members of the Democratic machine in a neighboring county, one Ben Southall, a reform candidate, had nearly been elected sheriff. Immediately after the election, the reformers came to Hills as one of the handful of Republican lawyers in the area, and he filed a sensational complaint in State circuit court within two weeks, asking that the election results be set aside. His complaint alleged that election officials conspired with the machine candidate and spent approximately $50,000 on election day "for the purpose to buy or steal for him enough votes to make his election a certainty." In three rural townships which gave the machine candidate twice his margin of victory, Hills alleged there had been "open, notorious and gross fraud" and no provisions for secret balloting: in Randolph, an election official marked voters' ballots for the machine candidate, then the voters were paid; in Solo, Southall voters were intimidated when a man ran at citizens "with a 4 by 4 timber, cussing and swearing," ordering them out because the polling place "was private property and they were trespassers"; in Gilt Edge, two election officials personally "assisted" with one-third of the ballots cast and money changed hands outside the polling place. Hills threw himself enthusiastically into the case, spending hundreds of hours on back roads tracking down witnesses. He was disbelieving when older colleagues told him that the elderly, distinguished circuit judge was so close to the machine that he would never render judgment for Southall. Hills fought through demurrers, dismissals and appeals, going twice to the State Supreme Court. He presented 65 witnesses to sustain the allegations of his complaint. After two years of legal delays, the circuit judge dismissed his case because it was already time for the next election anyway. The State Supreme Court had the last word: "While we approve the sincerity, zeal and resourcefulness of counsel for Southall, it is our firm opinion that this case has become moot from the passage of time." It was, says John Hills, "enough to make a cynic out of anybody."

In Memphis, Hills encountered gross pollution for the first time: in a sailboat race he once had to tack around a dead cow floating, belly-up, in a dammed-up reach of the Mississippi. He became a founding officer of the Memphis Environmental Action Committee, which put public pressure on big local polluters like the Velsicol Chemical Corporation, identified by Donald Mount as the source of the lower Mississippi River fish kill. Hills and his wife separated in 1970, and he wound up in Washington trying water pollution cases for the Natural Resources Division of the Department of Justice. In 1971 and 1972, Hills tried and won both of the Division's major pollution abatement suits — one of them the case of *United States of America* v. *Armco Steel Corporation* on the Houston Ship Channel. After watching the post-trial negotiations ordered by the White House in that case, he refused to sign the new decree which the government and Armco entered at the United States District Court. Colleagues learned to accept it as a matter of course when a conference would end abruptly with Hills being thrown out of a superior's office. One such superior, Walter Kiechel, recalls Hills as "pretty free-wheeling — an aggressive guy. But, to the extent we had differences, he always disagreed with good humor and class."

Thomas Truitt of EPA had in mind Hills' record as a tough litigator who harbored no false hopes for human nature, when he urged that Hills' superiors assign him to try the *Reserve Mining* case. Beginning in November 1972, Hills could often be found preparing for the trial, surrounded by the reports of Reserve's scientific consultants, cheerfully thumbing through *How to Lie with Statistics*. His cynicism did not stop with Reserve Mining Company. Although he was nominally a Republican, Hills once jokingly proposed forming the only kind of political party he could wholeheartedly support, the "Outists." The program of the party would be to throw out whoever was in office; the sole qualification for party membership would be a promise not to serve if elected. One of his major pre-trial concerns, Hills recalls, was to make sure "that political appointees did not keep the trial lawyers from prevailing in court." He adds matter-of-factly, "We all knew it was a corrupt administration." Verna Mize called him almost as soon as he was assigned to the case. He did not give her the usual bureaucratic brush-off. "I realized right away," he says, "that she could be useful" in keeping up Congressional pressure and preventing a sell-out. Assuming he could get *United States of America* v. *Reserve Mining Company* to trial, Hills was clear about his trial strategy. "Our position would be that Lake Superior was nearly perfect and that any change in the lake had to be bad," he says. "It was a position of necessity. We couldn't make a case by balancing plusses and minuses like the old Public Health Service types used to do." Thus, Hills adopted the philosphical position of the environmental activists at the outset. Verna Mize wrote to him warmly that he would be the environmentalists' David, saving their "shining Big-Sea-Water" from the Philistine giant, Reserve Mining Company.

During 1972, Reserve spent approximately $630,000 on lawyers and consultants to defend itself. And Reserve returned approximately $14,900,000 in after-tax profits to Armco and Republic Steel .

V

Troubled Dreams

Gary Glass was promoting another of his ambitious research projects in the summer of 1970 when he had lunch at a Duluth soda fountain with his boss, Donald Mount, and another scientist from the National Water Quality Laboratory. Glass talked about the advantages of conducting a series of chemical analyses of drinking water supplies for the presence of cancer-causing agents. The third scientist mentioned some scientific papers that showed extraordinarily high rates of cancer among workers who were exposed, not to chemicals, but to mineral particles in the manufacture of asbestos products. Glass recalled that the laboratory had traced submicroscopic particles of cummingtonite-grunerite, a mineral of the amphibole group, to the water supplies of Duluth and other communities on the Minnesota shore of Lake Superior from Reserve Mining Company's discharge of taconite tailings into the lake. He asked if cummingtonite-grunerite was related to asbestos, a type of mineral which separates into long, flexible, heat-resistant, corrosion-resistant fibers. The third scientist, who had done some post-graduate work in mineralogy, explained that asbestos was a non-scientific name for a mineral called chrysotile of the serpentine group, unrelated to amphiboles. At that time, nearly all — well over 95% — of the asbestos products in the United States were manufactured from chrysotile.

•   •   •

In 1970 Dr. Irving J. Selikoff was a chest physician and professor at Mount Sinai School of Medicine in New York City. A stout, white-haired man with a warm smile and an easy bedside manner, he had won the Lasker Award of the American Public Health Association for his work during the years after World War II in developing Isoniazid, one of the drugs that have nearly eradicated tuberculosis in this country. In 1954, Dr. Selikoff turned from his work on tuberculosis to a study of a type of lung scarring called asbestosis. The patients in his study were a group of 230 factory workers. All of these men worked at a plant which had, until 1954, manufactured asbestos products for the Navy in Paterson, New Jersey. The asbestos products had been made, not from the most commonly-used mineral chrysotile, but from a type of amphibole, called amosite.

Slowly, Dr. Selikoff realized that his study of lung scarring was getting nowhere because the workers were dying of cancer before they could develop asbestosis. Dr. Selikoff and his colleagues made elaborate statistical studies and, by 1971, they reached some firm scientific conclusions. Their paper "Carcinogenicity of Amosite Asbestos" announced to the scientific and medical world that "Occupational exposure to amosite asbestos can be associated with serious cancer hazard." They reported that 25 of the workers in their study had died of lung cancer, where only three deaths from lung cancer would be expected in the same number of men of the same age in the general population. Five of the workers had died of mesothelioma, a diffuse, invariably fatal cancer of the lining of the chest or abdomen — a cancer so rare that virtually no such deaths would be expected in the general population. And there were five deaths from cancer of the gastrointestinal tract, where less than two would be expected. The work of Dr. Selikoff and his colleagues conclusively demonstrated that amphibole asbestos, as well as chrysotile asbestos, could cause cancer. Shortly after he started his study of the Paterson workers, Dr. Selikoff also began to study a larger group of insulation workers exposed to chrysotile asbestos; he found similar increases in cancer rates there, as had a number of researchers studying exposure to chrysotile.

• • •

Dr. Reuben R. Merliss, a physician practicing internal medicine in Beverly Hills, California, had read a number of Dr. Selikoff's articles in the course of treating people who worked with asbestos. Dr. Merliss recalls waiting for his wife to buy produce in a Japanese market one day. He was standing next to some sacks of rice. His eye was drawn to a warning on the labels of the sacks: COATED WITH GLUCOSE AND TALC. WASH CAREFULLY. He knew from his reading that talc is often contaminated with both chrysotile and amphibole asbestos. He also knew from Dr. Selikoff's work that asbestos workers showed marked increases in gastrointestinal cancer, especially stomach cancer. And he knew that Japan had one of the highest rates of stomach cancer in the world. Dr. Merliss decided to buy a sack of rice and send a sample to a nearby laboratory for microscopic analysis. The laboratory reported that, as he suspected, the rice contained measurable quantities of particles which looked like asbestos. In September 1971, Dr. Merliss published a short, carefully documented article in *Science* magazine suggesting that asbestos-contaminated talc on rice is the carcinogen responsible for the high rate of Japanese stomach cancer.

• • •

In her efforts to generate public opposition to Reserve Mining Company's dumping of taconite tailings into Lake Superior, Verna Mize worked particularly hard on the United Automobile Workers. The UAW figured to be her natural ally, since it was a liberal union with its own department of conservation and many members who vacationed near Lake Superior. She spoke to a meeting of the UAW Community Action Program during 1972 and sent them one of her regular "battle reports" pointing out that citizens might take an effective stand against Reserve at a public hearing scheduled in Duluth on December 7, 1972, by the International Joint Commission. This Commission, composed of representatives of the governments of the United States and Canada, had vaguely defined powers to look into water quality in the Great Lakes. After several telephone calls between Mrs. Mize and the UAW staff, the union committed itself to oppose Reserve's discharge at the International Joint Commission hearing. The union invited a number of environmental organizations to attend a planning session in Duluth the night before the hearing. One of the organizations invited was the Northern Environmental Council. The staff director of the Council was unable to attend the planning session, but he asked Dr. Joseph Mengel, a Professor of Geology at the Wisconsin State College in Superior, just across the harbor from Duluth, if he'd be interested in going as a substitute. When Mengel arrived at the planning session, it was already under way.

The UAW planning session is still a vivid memory for one of the environmentalists who was there, the president of the Save Lake Superior Association, Mrs. Arlene Lehto. (Arlene Lind Harvell had recently married Richard Lehto, the owner of a small rubber stamp and print shop in Duluth. With characteristic enthusiasm she enlisted her husband in the cause. Grant Merritt of the Minnesota Environmental Control Citizens Association had recruited three law students to investigate the Reserve Mining controversy. Charles Stoddard of the Northern Environmental Council had seen to it that their investigative work, which raised a number of questions about the good faith and tactics of Reserve and its allies, was turned into a 200-page report. Using borrowed equipment and volunteer help, working at night, the Lehtos printed 1,000 copies of the report and sold them through the Save Lake Superior Association, under the title *Superior Polluter*.)

Arlene Lehto recalls that Joseph Mengel sat in the UAW planning session for about half an hour before he said, "I guess I misunderstood what this meeting was about." His interest was controlling the erosion of red clay banks on the Wisconsin shore of Lake Superior, not stopping the discharge of Reserve Mining Company. (In fact, the company was shortly to retain him as a consultant.) He apologized for interrupting the meeting and started to leave. Mrs. Lehto walked him to the door. There, Mengel pulled out a Xerox copy of the *Science* article by Dr. Merliss, "Talc-Treated Rice and Japanese Stomach Cancer." He showed her a photomicrograph in the article. Someone, he said, should be looking into the similarity of these needle-like particles and mineral particles found in Reserve Mining Company's discharge. As Mengel spoke, Mrs. Lehto quickly wrote technical terms on the back of a file folder she was carrying: "asbestos, chrysotile, amphibole, cummingtonite-grunerite."

After the planning session was over, Mrs. Lehto began to worry about what Mengel had told her. For more than a year, she recalls, she had been bothered by a dream which often recurred several nights in a row. In the dream, she walked through the City of Duluth, its buildings surrealistically white and angular. Around her people fell dead on the sidewalks. It seemed that something invisible, indefinable, was coming from Lake Superior. At home, Mrs. Lehto told her son about her dream and what Mengel had said. Together, they looked through a dictionary for the words she had written down. Her speech for the International Joint Commission hearing was already written. She decided she'd better add a paragraph to it.

On the morning of December 7, 1972, Mrs. Lehto spoke to the Commission hearing. Her speech was, for the most part, predictable. Among other things, she reiterated the philosophy of the Save Lake Superior Association and entered a copy of *Superior Polluter* into the record. But she also reminded the Commission that particulate matter identified as taconite tailings was present in the water supply of Duluth and "we drink it, we consume it." She went on:

> The Japanese have only recently discovered that the asbestos used in the grinding process for their rice may be a cancer-producing agent. The character of taconite tailings also includes the same fibrous amphibole. To our knowledge, no one has even suspected that this might be a cancer-producing agent. And because historically the burden of proof has rested not with the

polluter, but with the victim, our daily ingestion of
polluted water will continue — perhaps until too late.

Members of the International Joint Commission asked Mrs. Lehto
a few polite questions about the Save Lake Superior Association
at the conclusion of her speech, and went on to other matters.

•   •   •

One of the people in the audience during Mrs. Lehto's
speech was Philip Cook of the National Water Quality Laboratory. During the summer of 1972, Gary Glass hired Cook, who
had just been awarded his Ph.D. in inorganic chemistry, to
familiarize himself with every study of Lake Superior that had
ever been done by Reserve Mining Company, the government, or
independent researchers, and to guide the government's lawyers in
building a scientifically sound case against Reserve. Cook was the
descendant of a long line of taciturn New Englanders. An amateur
hockey player and aggressive downhill skier, he had begun
flycasting for trout when he was 12 and still enjoyed getting up
before dawn to stand fishing in a cold stream in raw weather.
After college, Cook joined the Air Force and served as a nuclear
weapons control officer in Turkey. His experience overseas and
the war in Vietnam had combined, he says, to change him from
"a conservative who blindly accepted the way things are — I'd
read Rachel Carson's *Silent Spring* in college and thought she was
an alarmist — to a totally questioning person." While in graduate
school, he represented environmentalists on Wisconsin Governor
Patrick Lucey's Committee on the Use of Fish Toxicants. Cook
also had a concern about pollution of the human environment akin
to hypochondria. Upon his arrival in Duluth, he began gathering
and absorbing file cabinets full of data on Reserve's discharge.
When Reserve's lawyers would demand the government's
computer program for its data on the case, Federal lawyers would
smile and point at Cook. Since the identification and measurement
of Reserve's tailings by x-ray diffraction underlay the govern-

ment's entire scientific case, Cook also took personal charge of that work, performing a rigorous series of experiments to lower limits of detection and improve the accuracy of mineral identification and precision of measurements.

With his usual thoroughness, Cook made notes on Mrs. Lehto's speech. He discussed the speech with his supervisor at the laboratory, Gary Glass. Cook thought that Mrs. Lehto's remarks were "irresponsible"; Glass dismissed them as "unfounded." ("If only she'd mentioned that article," Cook laments.) The week following Mrs. Lehto's speech, Cook began taking daily samples of Duluth tap water with a pressure filtration tank; since he had a mountain of other work to do, he used his evenings and weekends to analyze the samples by x-ray diffraction, identifying Reserve's tailings in each sample by the presence of the amphibole mineral cummingtonite-grunerite. He wasn't examining tap water specifically because of Mrs. Lehto's speech, he recalls, but because it was a good way to keep track of what happened to concentrations of tailings in Lake Superior during the winter.

By the spring of 1973, Cook was under a great deal of pressure. Scientific reports prepared for the Federal government and for Reserve Mining Company were overflowing his filing cabinets and bookshelves. More and more of his time was consumed in bringing the laboratory's x-ray diffraction work up to his own exacting standards. As the trial date approached, lawyers' questions and pleas for help multiplied. He also had a wife and family to support, and his temporary appointment as a government employee was about to expire. No one had found any money to extend it. In the first week of May, Cook went to Colorado, where he'd taken his master's degree, to look for work. He ran into the professor who had taught him x-ray diffraction at the Colorado School of Mines, and told him how he was using x-ray diffraction to monitor levels of cummingtonite-grunerite in the Duluth water supply. The professor said he'd recently read that particles of another amphibole mineral, actinolite-tremolite, could cause lung cancer. What, he wondered, would be the effect of drinking such particles? Cook now recalled a conversation of the previous month at a meeting of lawyers and government consultants at the National Water Quality Laboratory. At that time,

Professor James Kramer of Canada's McMaster University expressed concern about airborne dust from Reserve Mining Company's operations; he said that some amphibole particles could cause lung cancer. When Cook returned to Duluth, Gary Glass was able to tell him that his temporary appointment had been extended. In his turn, Cook told Glass that he was now concerned about the cancer-causing potential of tailings in Duluth's drinking water. But the two men were almost immediately distracted by other demands on their time.

On the morning of Monday, May 21, Gary Glass went directly to Cook's office when he came into work. He'd had a dream that night, he said, that he shouldn't drink the Duluth water. Cook should drop everything else and go to work on the cancer question right away. Cook went downstairs to the library of the National Water Quality Laboratory. By the end of the morning, he had read Dr. Merliss' article "Talc-Treated Rice and Japanese Stomach Cancer" and Dr. Selikoff's article "Carcinogenicity of Amosite Asbestos." He turned to a mineralogical text. He learned that "amosite" was not a scientific term, but a trade name derived from "Asbestos Mines of South Africa." The proper mineralogical name for amosite was cummingtonite-grunerite, the same mineral that was the major constituent of Reserve's tailings. "When I read this, the hair stood up on the back of my neck," Cook says. He and Glass began a computer search of published reports on amphiboles, asbestos, and cancer. Cook told his wife what he'd learned. "We can't drink that water," he said, "but don't tell anyone or they'll think I'm foolish."

On Friday, May 25, John Hills, the Federal government's chief lawyer in the *Reserve Mining* case, was in Duluth consulting with an expert witness from the West Coast. Cook gathered the literature he had found and approached Hills. He did so cautiously. Hills was exhausted. He had been travelling almost constantly for six months, taking pretrial depositions and interviewing experts. Now, with trial only 70 days away, Cook might be asking him to start preparing a whole new case. Cook waited patiently while Hills and his expert talked about conspiracy theories of official involvement in John F. Kennedy's assassination (a preoccupation, well known to his associates, that was symptomatic of Hills' cynical, anarchistic view of government). Finally, Cook told Hills what he had learned over the last week. To Cook's relief, Hills listened carefully, seemed to understand, and told Cook he and Glass should consult some experts during the next week, while he (Hills) was taking his vacation for the year on Cape Cod with his daughter. During the following week Cook and Glass, together with an attorney from the EPA's litigation office in Washington, called cancer experts around the country. The experts confirmed that they were indeed on to a serious problem.

On Friday, June 1, Cook and Glass met their laboratory director, Donald Mount, who had just returned to town from a business trip. Cook approached Mount even more cautiously than he had Hills. He knew Mount was a skeptic about the case against Reserve and had long been at odds with Glass. "I couldn't believe we'd overlooked this," Cook says, "and I was afraid Mount would dismiss it as a half-baked idea." But Mount immediately took Cook and Glass very seriously. His only reservation, Mount says, was that "no one else is going to believe this." He asked for scientific literature to read overnight and said they should take the matter to Washington as soon as possible. Cook and Glass said that the EPA lawyer they'd been working with had already arranged for them to meet in Washington on Monday with cancer experts from Dr. Selikoff's laboratory at Mt. Sinai School of Medicine and from three Federal agencies.

On Monday, June 4, John Hills opened a meeting in a long, narrow conference room overlooking the Potomac River on the eleventh floor of the EPA headquarters building in Washington. Sitting next to Hills were two lawyers from the EPA litigation office, formerly headed by Thomas Truitt. Across the table from him were Mount, Glass and Cook. Thirty feet away at the end of the table were Dr. William J. Nicholson, a biophysicist and Assistant Professor of Community Medicine at Mt. Sinai School of Medicine, and three scientists (an experimental pathologist and two biochemists) representing the Department of Health, Education and Welfare, the Food and Drug Administration, and the National Cancer Institute. Hills asked Mount to chair the meeting.

Mount outlined the situation briefly. Gary Glass showed the scientists electron microscope photographs of needle-like amphibole particles in Reserve's tailings and in the Duluth water supply. Cook explained the approximate concentrations of particles in the water supply, as determined by x-ray diffraction. Mount asked the cancer experts for their assessment of the situation.

Nicholson spoke first, in rapid bursts, his thoughts often overtaking his words in mid-sentence. He pointed out that the concentrations reported by Cook would have to be confirmed by an electron microscope count; it appeared to be an enormous number of amphibole particles, he said, about a thousand times greater than any concentration of asbestos he'd ever seen in water. The Federal scientists spoke cautiously. The man from the Food and Drug Administration remarked that the workers who had contracted cancer from asbestos had been *inhaling* asbestos particles; there was no proof you could get cancer from *ingesting* asbestos, as people in Duluth were doing. Nicholson agreed there was no definitive scientific proof, but pointed out that Dr. Selikoff had studied groups of workers exposed to both amphibole and chrysotile asbestos, and he had found marked increases of gastro-intestinal cancer in both groups. The man from the National Cancer Institute said his experiments with rats suggested that relatively large needles, or fibers, of asbestos dust, longer than 20 microns (about one thousandth of an inch), seemed to be the most carcinogenic; most of the particles in the pictures of the Duluth water supply appeared to him to be much shorter. Nicholson replied that every needle-like particle of asbestos should be "treated with respect"; most of the particles which Dr. Selikoff had found in autopsy tissue from asbestos workers were less than *one* micron long. The man from the Food and Drug Administration summarized: drinking the amphibole particles in the Duluth water would create a health risk of undefined proportions.

The cancer experts then discussed ways in which the health risk to the people of Duluth could be better defined. The man from the National Cancer Institute estimated that a well-run rat experiment would take a couple of years, after it was set up. Studies of cancer rates in the population of Duluth wouldn't be very helpful at this stage, Nicholson said; Reserve had been discharging tailings for less than 17 years, and there was generally a lag of 20 years or more between the time a population was exposed to a carcinogen and the time significant differences in cancer rates appeared. Perhaps, Nicholson suggested, the Mt. Sinai School of Medicine could get autopsy tissue from the lymph nodes and the gastrointestinal tracts of people who died in Duluth; the number of particles in this tissue might then be compared with the number of particles in the tissue of asbestos workers who were known to have an increased risk of cancer.

Donald Mount was getting impatient. The Federal experts seemed to be "pussyfooting around," he recalls, and no one was proposing any action. Mount and his laboratory workers and their families had to decide whether or not to drink this water. Finally he interrupted the discussion: would the experts drink the water if they lived in Duluth? Three of the men at the end of the table said they wouldn't drink the water. Only the man from the National Cancer Institute said he would. Mount asked why. The man said he was too old to have to worry about getting cancer 20 years from now. Mount persisted: would he let his grandchildren drink the water? "Oh, no," he said. This was the first instance, Mount recalls, of something he was to see repeatedly in coming weeks: people would use a much greater standard of care to protect themselves and their families than to protect the public. On this note, the meeting broke up.

While this meeting was going on, John Hills' nine year-old daughter Mary Alice was playing eight floors below in the office of A. Gordon Everett, the chief scientific advisor in EPA's Office of Enforcement. Helped by a member of Everett's staff, Mary Alice drew a picture for her father of a murky gray waterfall of taconite tailings entering a clear, blue lake. Fish leaped from the lake crying "Help! I can't breathe." The picture epitomized the ecological case that EPA had carefully constructed against Reserve Mining Company. Neither Mary Alice Hills nor Gordon Everett had any idea that that case was now insignificant, in light of the newly-discovered risk to human health. The young lawyers from EPA's litigation office working with Hills and the Duluth scientists had decided not to tell Everett and the rest of the EPA hierarchy anything about their new evidence until the last possible minute. Once word was out, they thought, Everett was sure to insist on a complicated time-consuming scientific program under his direction, before the Agency made any decisions. Thomas Truitt, the lawyers' former boss, might have been able to manage Everett, but Truitt had left EPA a few months ago. (His lawyers were sure he intended to leave the government when Truitt showed up the morning after President Nixon's landslide re-election wearing a black arm band.) Lacking Truitt's chutzpah and politesse — qualities which junior officials must have to win bureaucratic struggles — the lawyers had decided to see for themselves whether responsible scientists concluded that Reserve Mining Company was creating a hazard to human health. They would find some way to present those conclusions to Judge Miles Lord, with or without the support of Everett and their superiors.

As a career EPA employee, Donald Mount was less cavalier about informing his superiors. After the June 4 meeting broke up, he enlisted the help of a friend in EPA headquarters to take things to the top. Within an hour, Mount, Glass and Cook were riding a private elevator to the top-floor office of John R. Quarles, Jr., who was now EPA's second-in-command as its Acting Deputy Administrator. (A month earlier, President Nixon, in an effort to revive his fading credibility, had transferred EPA's notoriously independent first Administrator, William Ruckelshaus, to the Department of Justice. As a result of this transfer, people in the EPA chain of command had temporarily moved up a notch.) Sitting at a coffee table in Quarles' outer office, Mount briefly outlined for Quarles the latest developments in the *Reserve Mining* case. His outline was too brief. Both Cook and Glass were startled when Quarles couldn't remember what lake Reserve Mining Company was on. Mount patiently explained the basic facts and talked earnestly for several more minutes, without apparent effect. Glass sums up Quarles' attitude as, "just another fire drill." Mount says, "I was dumbfounded — he didn't seem to care."

Crestfallen, Mount, Glass and Cook left their meeting with Quarles to fly back to Duluth. For the moment, they would sit tight and see what the lawyers could do. In the meantime, they decided they would all take drinking water for their families from a well on Mount's farm outside Duluth. Gary Glass' wife Fayth recalls explaining to her babysitter at this time that their drinking water was in bottles "because we're having trouble with the plumbing."

On Wednesday, June 6, John Hills went to the Mt. Sinai School of Medicine in New York City to see if Dr. Irving J. Selikoff would give him a witness statement setting forth his opinion on the risk posed to human health by the presence of taconite tailings in Duluth's drinking water. Under a pretrial order issued by Judge Lord, the lawyers for both sides in the *Reserve Mining* case were required to file in court a statement of the expected testimony of any prospective witness. A witness statement from Dr. Selikoff would become available not only to Reserve, but also to the Federal government's co-plaintiffs — the governments of the three States bordering Lake Superior and environmental groups such as the Save Lake Superior Association. Hills knew that the other plaintiffs would use this evidence even if the Federal bureaucracy tried to bury it. So Judge Lord would have to consider any risk to public health in deciding the case.

Dr. Selikoff was by now the country's leading authority on asbestos as a cause of human disease. "I think it's possible to be a very good physician without being involved with the fate of your patients," Dr. Selikoff says. But, he goes on, "it's a terrible thing to see someone die of cancer — heartbreaking. For the first time in history, we are learning the causes of this major disease. At the very least, we should try to prevent preventable disease and unhappiness." Dr. Selikoff has a willingness uncharacteristic of his profession to take strong public stands. He ridicules the idea of absolute impartiality in public health research by recalling Abraham Lincoln's story about the pioneer woman who came upon her husband struggling with a bear and called out, "Go to it husband! Go to it bear!" Some of Dr. Selikoff's scientific colleagues refer to him contemptuously as a "headline grabber," "a professional alarmist," and "the Ralph Nader of public health." "Irving works hard to be a good scientist," says Dr. Lawrence Plumlee, an EPA medical advisor. "But his moral goal as an

M.D. — to reduce illness — is stronger than that of most Ph.D. scientists. He's chosen to accept public controversy as the burden he has to bear to satisfy his sense of morality." Dr. Plumlee recalls visiting Mt. Sinai to discuss asbestos regulations. "Irving took me to see a patient who had mesothelioma — this man had worked with asbestos for three months 40 years ago, and now he had no chance of surviving. He took me to see that patient in order to influence my judgment. And it certainly did make me wonder about the morality of deciding to allow x number of tumors."

Hills spent the afternoon of June 6 talking to Dr. Selikoff, Nicholson, and several other Mt. Sinai staff members. "If our suspicions are correct," Dr. Selikoff told him, "there is a significant risk of cancer to the people of Duluth and there will be epidemiological studies until the year 2000." Dr. Selikoff thought the best way to check out these suspicions would be to follow up on Nicholson's suggestions: his laboratory would examine by electron microscope samples of Duluth drinking water and of Duluth autopsy tissues; they would also compare the number of amphibole particles found in Duluth tissue samples with the number of particles found in the tissues of asbestos workers who were known to have an increased risk of cancer. Dr. Selikoff agreed to serve as an expert witness without fee and dictated a one-page witness statement to Hills. It said:

> The medical profession has recently learned that mineral fibers in the size range of those present in the Duluth water supply may cause cancer. Indeed, mineral fibers related to species being discharged into Lake Superior have been found to cause cancer in man . . . . The potential hazard therefore involves possible serious human health effects. We have arranged for urgent studies to be done to seek initial data on this aspect of the question . . . . It is anticipated that the first meaningful results will be available for evaluation in two months.

The next day Hills and the EPA lawyers who had been working with him set out to get official clearance to file Dr. Selikoff's witness statement in court. They met at EPA headquarters to show a draft of the statement to Alan G. Kirk II, formerly John Quarles' deputy, now Acting Assistant Administrator for Enforcement. Kirk expressed concern about unnecessarily alarming the people of Duluth. Hills said he planned to file Dr. Selikoff's witness statement under the terms of Judge Lord's pretrial order, and that it was bound to become public knowledge. "Kirk finally nodded his head in agreement, probably without any very clear idea of what he was getting into," recalls one of the EPA lawyers. On Friday, June 8, John Hills discussed Dr. Selikoff's witness statement at the Department of Justice with Wallace H. Johnson, Jr., the politically-appointed Assistant Attorney General for Natural Resources, and Walter Kiechel, the senior civil servant of his division. Johnson, five years younger than Hills, had just arrived at this job from the White House staff. Johnson took a traditional view of the Justice Department's role in litigation. "We acted as a law firm," he says. "The job of our client agencies was to make environmental policy. Our job was to present that policy in court." Hills said that he already had the approval of EPA, the "client agency"— in the form of Alan Kirk's nod — to file Dr. Selikoff's statement. He also mentioned Judge Lord's pretrial order. Hills' superiors warned him not to file the statement publicly, but gave him permission to submit it at a closed session of the U.S. District Court.

Accompanied by Robert J. Sheran, a senior trial lawyer for Reserve Mining Company, John Hills handed a copy of Dr. Selikoff's witness statement to Judge Lord in his chambers at the Minneapolis Federal courthouse on Monday, June 11. Judge Lord read the statement while Sheran expressed his anger: it was incredible, Sheran said, that the Federal government would make such an irresponsible charge if it weren't desperate to win its lawsuit against his client. Judge Lord summoned lawyers for the other parties in the *Reserve Mining* case to his courtroom and posted a marshall to keep out the press and public. He had decided that it would be better to treat this information confidentially until everyone involved had an opportunity to reflect on it.

The judge turned to Grant Merritt, the Executive Director of the Minnesota Pollution Control Agency, and asked if he knew the subject of this hearing. There was a long silence. Merritt said no, but he had a guess. Judge Lord asked him to explain. The director of Merritt's Duluth office had attended the International Joint Commission hearing of December 7, 1972, and had discussed Arlene Lehto's speech with Merritt and a geologist on Merritt's staff afterwards. The geologist had checked some of his textbooks to confirm the outlines of her speech. Then the agency had retained a consultant to establish the presence of "asbestos-type minerals" in Reserve Mining Company's discharges not only into Lake Superior, but also through its stacks into the air. Merritt was even now awaiting the consultant's report.

Judge Lord seemed overwhelmed by these new developments. This could, he said, "potentially be the number one ecological disaster of our time." He held a series of closed hearings in his courtroom during the week of June 11. At one hearing, he took the extraordinary step of inviting another judge to sit behind the bench with him, explaining "you get sort of lonesome when you are all alone, with good lawyers on both sides and great public issues at stake." "He certainly had my sympathy," says William J. Williams, Executive Vice President of Republic Steel, who followed the case closely. "I was sure the public health issue weighed heavily on him." On June 11, Judge Lord gave the Federal bureaucracy a share of his burden: he cautioned that the weight which he gave to this new evidence would depend to some extent on how strongly the Federal government acted upon it. This remark destroyed the hope of John Hills and the EPA lawyers working with him that they could get Judge Lord to act on Dr. Selikoff's evidence in complete disregard of the EPA hierarchy. In closing, the judge instructed everyone assembled in his courtroom on June 11 not to talk to the press until he gave his approval.

After this hearing, a lawyer from EPA's litigation office flew from Minneapolis to Duluth for a late-night meeting in Donald Mount's office with Mount, Gary Glass and Philip Cook. The lawyer had learned that the EPA staff was meeting the next day in Washington with the Acting Administrator of the Agency,

Robert Fri, to decide to what to do about Reserve Mining Company and the Duluth water supply. None of the men gathered in Mount's office had been invited to meet with the Acting Administrator and no one had asked for their advice, but they thought Judge Lord's remarks made it urgent that EPA act. Michael Gross, another lawyer in EPA's litigation office, had agreed to present their views to the Acting Administrator. Over the course of several hours, the men drafted a two-page message and Telexed it to Washington. The message said that:

1. Fibers in the Duluth water supply which have been discharged by the Reserve Mining Company have the same mineralogical and morphological characteristics as amosite asbestos. [This statement adopted the position of Dr. Selikoff and Nicholson in the dispute over the size of asbestos particles most likely to produce cancer, without acknowledging the existence of any other position.]

2. The daily level of exposure to such fibers by a person using the Duluth water supply is one thousand times that of a person using any other water supply, and approaches occupational exposure levels. [This statement was based on admittedly sketchy data — Nicholson had just reported over the telephone his electron microscope count of amphibole particles in the first four Duluth water samples sent to him by Cook.]

3. Upon ingestion, such fibers pose a risk of increased incidence of cancers. [This statement rested on Dr. Selikoff's reports of increased rates of gastrointestinal cancer among asbestos workers, ignoring the lack of definitive scientific proof that exposure to asbestos particles *solely* by means of ingestion would cause cancer.]

Therefore, the exposure of citizens along the shores of Lake Superior to such fibers should be minimized by the following means . . . .

EPA should . . . cooperate with efforts to provide users of the affected water supplies with alternate sources of drinking water, *e.g.*, by trucking to convenient distribution points . . . .

EPA should ask the Department of Justice to seek a preliminary injunction immediately abating Reserve Mining Company's discharge to Lake Superior; this should reduce the amounts of fibers in affected water supplies approximately 5 to 20 times over the first month. [The estimated rate of clearing of the water was based on Cook's x-ray diffraction analysis of samples taken from Lake Superior when the Reserve plant had been closed for regularly-scheduled maintenance during the summer of 1972.]

All of the men in Mount's office were reluctant to recommend strong action against Reserve, knowing that such a recommendation would arouse political resistance. But Mount persuaded them that if EPA did not seek an immediate shut-down to protect public health in these circumstances, it would never be able to. Michael Gross carried this recommendation into the meeting with Acting Administrator Fri on June 12. A tall, balding man in his forties, Fri had a preference for listening over talking rare in the upper reaches of government. He had already announced his intention to return to his management consulting business rather than accept a permanent appointment as EPA Administrator. Although he knew he would only be in office a short time, he felt an obligation, he says, to make day-to-day regulatory decisions as they came up, and not to leave a mass of unfinished business for his successor. Gross recalls that Fri puffed reflectively on his pipe after he'd read the message from Mount's office, but that the reactions of John Quarles and his scientific advisor, Gordon Everett, were "incredulous." And Fri recalls that he looked primarily to Quarles and Everett for advice on what to do about Reserve Mining Company and the Duluth drinking water. Everett opposed immediate action against Reserve, first, because more research was necessary to prove that amphibole fibers in the water supplies of Duluth and the other affected communities came from Reserve. (The men in Mount's office would have laughed at this "necessary research"; they knew that five years of searching had not produced any credible evidence that there was a significant source of fibrous amphibole in Lake Superior other than Reserve.) Furthermore, Everett doubted there would be any positive effects from immediately shutting off Reserve's discharge: even if Reserve were the only source of amphibole fibers in Lake Superior, "a significant diminishment" of amphibole levels in the lake would not occur for "a decade to a century." (His projection was based, Everett says, on some "rough estimates" he'd made with members of his staff. It ignored the hard data developed by the men in Mount's office, showing the decline of amphibole levels in Lake Superior when Reserve had been closed for maintenance the previous summer. In retrospect, one of Everett's staff members concedes, their projection was "an overstatement.") John Quarles also argued against a preliminary injunction, which would necessarily close Reserve's plant while the company built on-land disposal facilities. "We had never sought to have a plant shut down," Quarles recalls, "with the exception of Armco Steel on the Houston Ship Channel — where we got into trouble." He had Everett prepare a study of the economic impact of closing Reserve: 3,000 people would be out of work; State and Federal tax losses would exceed $25 million in a year; the cost of unemployment compensation would exceed $4 million in the first six months; if Reserve's parent corporations turned to foreign sources of ore, more than $200 million would be added to the nation's annual balance of payments deficit.

Acting Administrator Fri says that these arguments by Everett and Quarles were the ones which swayed him on June 12. The meeting reached agreement that EPA should gather more data under Everett's direction. (Everett recalls that he proposed, in addition to his economic impact study, to retain some insurance actuaries to assess the risk to the affected population in Minnesota "on a worst case basis," but that John Quarles rejected the proposal on the grounds that such an assessment "might over-balance the decision-making process.") The "bottom line" was that EPA would issue a non-committal press release.

When Gross telephoned word of this decision to Duluth, Donald Mount decided he was flying to Washington, invited or not. Mount spent two days "making the rounds," in Washington, he recalls, looking for some way to turn the agency around. He found "a lot of misinformation — and Gordon Everett seemed to be the source. After I talked to Everett, I thought 'These guys will masticate it for months.' " Mount searched out an EPA medical advisor, Dr. Lawrence Plumlee, and "talked to him like a Dutch uncle." Dr. Plumlee recalls, "Mount communicated his concern quite effectively. He and his family and his friends were exposed to that water." Dr. Plumlee agreed to support Mount in an attempt to get EPA's Assistant Administrator for Research and Development, Dr. Stanley Greenfield, to intervene with Acting Administrator Fri. On the morning of June 15, Mount and Dr. Plumlee met with Greenfield, who had been a meteorologist and environmental scientist with RAND Corporation, the West Coast think tank, before coming to EPA. Mount did most of the talking. "I had the feeling Greenfield was quite negative at the start," Mount says. "But some emotion registered on his face when I told him the least the Agency could do, was warn people to get their kids off that water." Mount was hopeful when he left Greenfield to catch a plane for a hearing in Judge Lord's chambers.

Judge Lord had decided he couldn't keep the lid on the public health evidence any longer, but he had scheduled one last private hearing. Two dozen people — lawyers for all of the parties, several scientists and physicians, and an agitated Congressman John Blatnik, fresh from a meeting with Acting EPA Administrator Fri — crowded Judge Lord's chambers for the hearing. The judge asked Mount to summarize the situation. When he finished, Judge Lord asked him, "Are you drinking Duluth water now?" Mount's reply was a barely audible "No, sir." "Why not? Because of this?" Mount nodded, "Yes." Smiling, Judge Lord gently compared Mount's position to that of a corporate officer profiting on the stockmarket from insider information.

The judge announced that he had placed a call to Dr. Selikoff on his speaker phone, to see when Dr. Selikoff would have a definitive opinion on the existence of a hazard to public health. John Hills was startled. He had not spoken with Dr. Selikoff since he first met him on June 6. A few careless words now might destroy his case. In response to a long series of questions from Congressman Blatnik, Dr. Selikoff's genial, avuncular voice informed the crowd in Judge Lord's chambers, "If I had the opportunity I would not drink the Duluth water, with what I know. But this is a summary type of statement and not necessarily the kind that I should make in public." He cautioned that "we do not know" cancer will "necessarily" result from drinking the water. The results of his examination of Duluth autopsy tissues should provide some further guidance in a couple of weeks or so. In the meantime, some alternative for Duluth tap water should be provided for "newborn babies . . . who are not yet exposed." Mount interjected the first note of skepticism about the conclusiveness of the tissue studies to be performed at Mt. Sinai. Leaning close to the speaker on Judge Lord's desk, he said, "I have been in research enough, like you, to know very often it doesn't come out that clearly." What if the tissue study did not find amphibole fibers? Even "if it is equivocal," Dr. Selikoff replied, "you will be almost duty-bound to provide an alternate water supply." When Dr. Selikoff hung up, John Hills permitted himself a smile. He wrote in his diary, "My credibility was 100% on the line at this meeting and 100% substantiated."

Before the June 15 hearing in Judge Lord's chambers adjourned, Michael Gross entered to report that EPA had reached a decision. Acting Administrator Fri had attended a meeting earlier that day scheduled chiefly to approve the innocuous press release which had been drafted after his first meeting on Reserve Mining earlier in the week. One of the scientists who attended the June 15 meeting recalls, "There was a lot of talk about avoiding panic in a citizenry too ignorant to make decisions. Alan Kirk [the Acting Assistant Administrator for Enforcement] was strongest on this. His underlying message was 'Don't stir the political pot.'

'Prudence' was carrying the day. Then Stan Greenfield [the Assistant Administrator for Research and Development] got up out of his chair. He was very emotional. He yelled that this wasn't just a political decision. We were dealing with people." Greenfield says, "You're damned right I was emphatic. Out of five Assistant Administrators, I was the only one who wasn't a lawyer. These lawyers were all on the road somewhere else and concerned about the very short-term impact of their decisions. In the past, I'd been talked into supporting a lot of regulations with very weak technical bases, in order to meet statutory deadlines and 'keep the agency credible.' Here we came to a situation where we *knew* the human effects of asbestos — albeit by the air route, rather than water — and the agency wasn't going to take a stand." Greenfield's forceful argument prevailed. At his insistence, the innocuous press release was converted into a warning, to be made public the same day:

> The Environmental Protection Agency announced today that high concentrations of asbestos fibers have been discovered in the water supply of Duluth and several communities on the Minnesota shore of Lake Superior. The source of these fibers is believed to be the discharge of taconite by Reserve Mining Company, Silver Bay, Minnesota. While there is no conclusive evidence to show that the present drinking water supply in this area is unfit for human consumption, the Agency feels that prudence dictates that an alternative source be found for very young children. The Environmental Protection Agency will continue to evaluate the risk as more information becomes available.

The *St. Paul Dispatch* for the afternoon of June 15, 1973 carried a banner headline in a type size that usually proclaims the beginning or ending of a war: "ASBESTOS-TYPE FIBER FOUND IN DULUTH WATER."

VI

Waiting to Find the Smoking Gun

On the morning of August 1, 1973, Verna Mize stood alone in front of the Minneapolis Federal courthouse carrying a placard reading: "Lake Superior: Preserve It, Don't 'Reserve' It." She put her sign away at 9:00 and went inside to get one of the last remaining seats in the courtroom of Judge Miles Lord. The judge invited members of the press to take ring-side seats in the jury box and the clerk called the case of *United States of America* v. *Reserve Mining Company* for trial.

The testimony of Philip Cook of the National Water Quality Laboratory took up most of the first week of trial. An environmental lawyer describes Cook as an "impressive witness. To start with, he looked like an astronaut — trustworthy, loyal, all that. Then, he made it clear he was unflinchingly willing to go wherever the scientific evidence led him." Reporters who covered the trial call Cook "patient . . . thoroughly professional . . . earnest to a fault . . . the sharpest witness the government had." For the last year, Cook recalls, he had often been on the verge of physical illness because of "the dishonesty and corruption of Reserve's scientific case — it made me pessimistic about Man as a moral being." Now, on the stand presenting his own work, he felt relaxed and confident.

Cook covered in painstaking detail his mineralogical examination of samples. He methodically eliminated the possibility that there was any significant source of the amphibole mineral cummingtonite-grunerite in Lake Superior, other than Reserve Mining Company. None was reported in extensive mineralogical literature on the Lake Superior basin. He found none in tributary streams.

He found none in the older sediments of the lake bottom beneath the freshly-deposited surface layer. He found none in samples of suspended solids taken from the Duluth water intake before Reserve began operations. Concentrations of cummingtonite-grunerite suspended in the water of Lake Superior declined with time when the plant was closed for maintenance. Concentrations suspended in the lake, or settled on its bottom, declined with distance from the plant, although, he testified, taconite tailings had now spread as far as the waters of the State of Michigan. Saul Friedman of the *Detroit Free Press* looked up from his notes at this point and saw Verna Mize silently weeping in the audience. Cook explained, on the basis of his reading of the mineralogical literature and of his own examination of samples by electron microscope, x-ray diffractometer, and infrared spectrometer, that much of the particulate matter discharged by Reserve was indistinguishable from amosite asbestos. He concluded: "My opinion is that there is amphibole asbestos present" in the Duluth water supply. "There is absolutely no doubt in my mind that [it] came from Reserve Mining Company. I studied the rivers. I studied the historical samples. The whole pattern of the lake after many years of study indicates that that could be the only possible source."

The United States took seven weeks to present its case against Reserve. Since the company was admitting nothing, John Hills put on the stand a parade of chemists, oceanographers, geologists, mineralogists, and microscopists to corroborate every aspect of Cook's testimony. Then, in September Hills presented four expert witnesses to establish the government's position on the risk to public health created by Reserve Mining Company. Hills selected these four witnesses from a short list proposed by Dr. Selikoff, and Hills worked with them to shape their testimony. Lawyers at the corporate headquarters of Armco and Republic read and analyzed the trial transcripts daily, and Reserve's trial lawyers, Edward Fride and Robert Sheran, met monthly with the chief executive officers of Armco Steel and Republic Steel to discuss strategy. Hills had never been in the same room with the Attorney General or the Administrator of the Environmental Protection Agency, much less discussed the *Reserve Mining* trial with them. When the secretary shared by all the plaintiffs' attorneys fell behind in mailing out trial transcripts, there were no complaints from Washington, and for a good reason — no one in Washington was reading the transcripts. "In government," explains a senior EPA official, "issues don't get attention and decisions don't get made, unless there's a gun at your head." So long as he did not file any formal pleadings or motions which would have required his superiors' approval, John Hills (and through him, Dr. Irving Selikoff) defined the government's position in *United States of America* v. *Reserve Mining Company* essentially without supervision or review.

William Nicholson of Mt. Sinai School of Medicine took the stand at the beginning of September. Forty years old, Nicholson, like Cook, had worked with nuclear weapons in the Air Force. After his military service, he became a committed liberal in politics. (He met Dr. Selikoff in 1966 when the latter had held a fund raising party at his home to support Nicholson's anti-war campaign for the Democratic Congressional nomination in northern New Jersey.) Nicholson's dedication to preventive medicine as a social goal sustained him through hundreds of hours of uncompensated overtime work on Reserve's discharge.

He testified that he had identified concentrations of 17 million to 74 million amphibole fibers per liter of water in electron microscope examinations of samples drawn from Duluth taps. He also identified similar concentrations of amphibole fibers in the water supplies of the towns of Beaver Bay and Two Harbors on the Minnesota shore of Lake Superior and of the City of Superior, Wisconsin (which occasionally tapped off the suburban Duluth system to supplement its regular supply of well water). It was difficult, he said to reconstruct the number of fibers which amphibole asbestos workers studied by Dr. Selikoff had inhaled, coughed up, and then swallowed. As a rough estimate, he calculated that they had swallowed approximately the same number of fibers in the course of four years on the job as people would swallow if they lived in Duluth or the other affected communities for 20 years. This was alarming, he pointed out, because asbestos workers with only four years on the job had abnormally high rates of cancer.

Nicholson testified that Dr. Selikoff's laboratory at Mt. Sinai had during the summer conducted an examination by electron microscope of the tissues of three people who had recently died in Duluth. They had found a handful of amphibole fibers, with only a very few outside the lungs. They had not examined any of the Duluth tissue which they had received since then. Reserve attacked Mt. Sinai's findings as statistically insignificant. But Nicholson testified that Mt. Sinai had only recently begun to examine tissue from asbestos workers other than lung tissue. It turned out that it was very difficult to find asbestos fibers outside of the lungs — even in those workers who were known to have high rates of gastrointestinal cancer. The problem was compounded by the extremely small field of vision of the electron microscope. (A witness for Reserve later testified that it would take about 9,000 years, using a quarter-million dollar electron microscope 24 hours a day, seven days a week, to examine enough ultra-thin slices of human tissue to total one cubic centimeter.) Robert Sheran questioned Nicholson for Reserve. His voice taut with emotion, Sheran asked, "Wouldn't you say that it's a reasonable proposition that before you characterize an activity as constituting a serious public health hazard, that somebody, somewhere, should establish that one death or serious illness is attributable to the activity?" Nicholson responded:

> I would think that that would be highly irresponsible, particularly in circumstances where the disease and death that might be occasioned from such exposure are a long time in coming. If we wait until we see the bodies in the street, we would then be certain that there would be another thirty or forty years of mortality experience that would be before us. We would have built up a backlog of disease over which we have little control.

Nicholson testified that Reserve was polluting not only the water, but also the air. He had examined air samples, which he'd taken near the Reserve plant at Silver Bay for the Minnesota Pollution Control Agency; his examination revealed quantities of airborne amphibole fibers in the same range as the quantities of fibers found in the air of asbestos workers' homes. This was ominous, because Dr. Selikoff had recently begun to study the wives and children of men who had worked with asbestos 20 years earlier and had found the first x-ray symptoms of asbestos exposure to be widespread among them. After this testimony, the United States joined Minnesota in amending its complaint to allege that Reserve's emissions into the air, as well as the water, created a nuisance condition which Judge Lord should order abated. The State also alleged that Reserve was violating its Air Pollution Control Regulation 17, which the Minnesota Pollution Control Agency had adopted in 1972 (with the technical assistance of William Nicholson) to limit strictly asbestos air pollution.

Nicholson was followed as a witness by Dr. Harold Stewart, 74, recently retired after 30 years as the chief pathologist of the National Cancer Institute. In private, Dr. Stewart expressed disbelief that the Federal government could be carrying on a highly publicized billion-dollar "war against cancer" without acting to prevent human exposure to suspected or known cancer-causing agents. On the witness stand, he reviewed the contamination of Duluth's drinking water and warned:

> I think it's a carcinogen introduced into the environment of the population exposed to these water supplies . . . You give it to the infants, to . . . those that are already ill . . . including those who, as we must suspect from animal experimentation, are more susceptible to cancer than others . . . this is a captive population . . . . [I]f you want to preserve the situation that produces that, then you will definitely condemn certain people to death.

On cross-examination, Edward Fride for Reserve suggested that it might be better to defer any action until the completion of the tissue studies proposed by Dr. Stewart's good friend, Dr. Selikoff, now also being conducted by experts for Reserve. Dr. Stewart answered:

>This is a fine experiment and this experiment should
>be done as well as many other experiments on this
>population of Duluth, because this is a wonderful
>opportunity now for medicine and science to study the
>exposure of a captive population to a known car-
>cinogen in the domestic water supply over a certain
>period of years. When the atomic bomb was blasted in
>Hiroshima, the Japanese and Americans have studied
>this ever since . . . that is taking advantage of a human
>experiment . . . . I do not think it's necessary to with-
>hold the deletion of these carcinogens from the water
>until this experiment is done.

Attacking Dr. Stewart's assertion that there was a known carcinogen in Duluth's water supply, Fride suggested that even Dr.
Selikoff acknowledged there was no proof asbestos made from
cummingtonite-grunerite would cause cancer. Fride read Dr.
Stewart the first sentences of Dr. Selikoff's article. "Carcinogenicity of Amosite Asbestos": "Few data exist concerning the
comparative neoplastic potential in man of the several kinds of
asbestos. In particular, there has been no evidence concerning
whether the amosite variety is carcinogenic." Dr. Stewart
attempted to read from the body of the article, which supplied the
data previously lacking. Fride interrupted, "You've had a lot of
experience in writing articles for the scientific literature. Do you
and others . . . tend, in the first paragraph or so, to give a summary of what the contents of the article contains?" "Well, let me
see one of my articles," Dr. Stewart said. He fumbled through a
stack of literature, producing an article he'd written in 1931 —
one of the first clinical demonstrations of asbestosis published in
America. "The first sentence in this asbestos article is that asbestos, as such, was known to Pliny . . . . The next one was 'Charle-
magne was said to have possessed a tablecloth made of it which
was cleansed by passing through fire.' Now, that was one of my
articles . . . and that's no summary of the case."

Fride's cross-examination made more progress on other
fronts. Dr. Stewart had suffered a stroke after his retirement. His
head began to droop to the right as the day wore on, and Dr.

Stewart would hold his head upright by locking his left arm over the top of it. Fride drew from Dr. Stewart a long list of suspected carcinogens, many of them common in the human environment. Fride asked rhetorically if Dr. Stewart's wish to eliminate all of these agents from the environment "doesn't postulate in favor of returning to the caveman stage?" Implicit in this line of questioning was the suggestion that the risk created by Reserve's dumping of taconite tailings into Lake Superior had to be compared to the risks which society tolerates from all sorts of other human activities. But Reserve was barred from developing this implication by its steadfast insistence that its activities created no risk whatever.

The third public health expert to testify was Joseph K. Wagoner, a young Harvard Ph.D. in epidemiology, employed by the National Institute of Occupational Safety and Health at the Department of Health, Education and Welfare. In a business-oriented Administration, Wagoner had earned a reputation as a "whistle blower" about unhealthy working conditions. He sometimes had the furtive, hunted look of a man who is unsure how much he can reveal without being disciplined. Wagoner testified that epidemiological studies conducted in Canada, England, Finland, South Africa, and the United States demonstrated that exposure to the dust of chrysotile asbestos and of amphibole asbestos (including varieties made from the amphibole minerals anthophyllite, crocidolite and actinolite-tremolite, as well as cummingtonite-grunerite) could cause cancer of the lungs, cancer of the gastrointestinal tract and diffuse cancer of the lining of the chest and abdomen (mesothelioma) in humans. Furthermore, he said, nothing in world literature indicated a safe level of exposure to asbestos dust, below some theoretical "threshold" needed to cause cancer. In fact he was directing a study of lung cancer among workers employed only briefly in a relatively clean plant manufacturing asbestos products, which suggested "that there may be no threshold for the induction of respiratory tract malignancies."

Dr. Irving Selikoff took the stand on September 18. He testified for four days, showing hundreds of slides of disease statistics and of chest x-rays and malignant tissue specimens from dozens of individual patients — asbestos workers, their families and neighbors. His testimony demonstrated to those who watched and listened Dr. Selikoff's complete mastery of every aspect of the field; and it gave them an appreciation of the disease caused by asbestos, not only as a subject of medical research, but as an immediate human problem. He warned on the basis of America's experience with cancers caused by cigarettes, that medical science was only beginning to discover the tragic dimensions of cancers caused by asbestos. As late as the 1930's, he testified, lung cancer was still so rare that "only one physician in the United States saw even a few cases a year and he was doing practically all of the bronchoscopies for the country. The reason is, Your Honor, that lung cancer associated with cigarette smoking has a very long incubation period . . . . We didn't become a nation of cigarette smokers until after the First World War. Some people believe that this is the result of the millions of cartons of cigarettes that the American Red Cross sent to our doughboys overseas . . . . But in any case we didn't suspect what was going to happen as a result of cigarette smoking." Now lung cancer was the commonest of all cancers among men. It killed 200 Americans every day, and the rate of lung cancer was still going up. Most of the cancers associated with asbestos that had been seen to date were the result of exposure to asbestos before 1930, Dr. Selikoff testified. Up until then only five million tons of asbestos had been produced in recorded history. "We are now producing five million tons in one year and such disease as may be associated with this asbestos will not be seen until the year 2000, 2010, and 2020." He said that documented cases of mesothelioma in the absence of some identifiable exposure to asbestos are extremely rare. In the last 15 years the number of documented cases of mesothelioma in South Africa and Great Britain, two early world leaders in mining and milling of asbestos, had already increased ten-fold. Dr. Selikoff had never seen a patient recover from mesothelioma — no medical treatment had been successful. John Hills asked him to describe what it was like to die of mesothelioma. Judge Lord abruptly cut him off: "I don't need a description of how a patient feels when he has cancer . . . . We've all seen enough of that so we can use our own imagination." A man who knows the judge says, "He's one of the most highly developed hypochondriacs I've ever known. He was just sick during Dr. Selikoff's testimony."

On the afternoon of September 20, Dr. Selikoff concluded his direct testimony by stating his long-awaited opinion as to whether Reserve Mining Company was creating a hazard to public health. Dr. Selikoff acknowledged the absence of definitive scientific proof that exposure to asbestos fibers by means of swallowing alone would cause cancer. It was, however, "highly probable" that the increased rates of gastrointestinal cancer which he and other researchers had observed in asbestos workers were the result of coughing up and swallowing asbestos fibers. Two clinical experiments with rats suggested that asbestos fibers placed in the stomach are soon disseminated beyond the walls of the gastrointestinal tract, but not necessarily to the tissues Dr. Selikoff had proposed to study in June. John Hills asked if the amphibole fiber concentrations which Nicholson had reported in the Duluth water supply created a hazard. Dr. Selikoff answered that there was "a distinct public health hazard." He continued: "We will not know whether or not these particular circumstances will cause cancer until . . . at least 25 to 35 years. This is in my opinion a form of Russian roulette and I don't know where the bullet is located." He said that it was an added cause of concern that Duluth residents were exposed to amphibole fibers in the water supply not only by ingestion, but also by inhalation near such conveniences as home laundries, air conditioners and room humidifiers. (Fayth Glass says: "Our son had a lot of respiratory problems as a baby. Until he was five, he used to stand and inhale above a cold mist humidifier every morning. It makes me sick to think about it.") Dr. Selikoff went on to testify that inhalation of the concentrations of amphibole fibers reported by Nicholson in the air of Silver Bay created "a particular hazard," and would probably result in deaths. Hills asked if the location of U.S. Highway 61 between the Reserve plant and the town of Silver Bay had any importance. "It certainly does," Dr. Selikoff replied. "I think we ought to have a sign at the entrance of . . . the town, 'Please Close Your Windows Before Driving Through.' I certainly would want to close mine."

The next morning Hills picked Dr. Selikoff up at his hotel to drive him to the Federal courthouse. Dr. Selikoff told Hills that the coverage of his testimony on the TV news last night had disturbed him. He thought that some of his remarks were being interpreted in a way that could create unnecessary despair among the people who lived along the Minnesota shore of Lake Superior. While he did not want to change the substance of his direct testimony, he had made some notes after watching the news and he would like the chance to qualify some of those remarks before his cross-examination began. He explained just what he wanted to say. Hills swallowed hard and said, "I'd rather you didn't, but do what you have to do."

In court, Hills asked Dr. Selikoff if he had decided that any points in his direct testimony needed clarification. Dr. Selikoff answered, "yes, sir." He briefly discussed the limitations of one of the rat experiments he had mentioned in his previous testimony, and said that he had not meant to impugn the integrity of any of the industry doctors whose work he had criticized. Then he came to his main points. "First of all my rather facetious remark about car windows in Silver Bay was, of course, not to be taken literally. I don't think I'd put my windows up . . . . I just wanted to emphasize that there is a community air pollution there of a different order of magnitude than Duluth." He went on to say that he did *not* consider that general community air pollution by asbestos in Duluth had been "shown at this time one way or the other to be or not to be . . . a public health problem." Finally, he said that it was his opinion "we have caught this problem in time, that if further contamination and exposure of Duluth or other communities of a similar nature is stopped or controlled, I think we can look forward, with some good confidence, to the future . . . . [W]e can, by limiting the duration of exposure and by limiting the intensity of exposure repeatedly — that we can minimize the cancer effect that may be associated." As soon as Dr. Selikoff finished talking, Judge Lord called a brief recess. "It's amazing," he told the lawyers for both sides. "It's like a movie running backwards. He's taking back everything he said yesterday." Hills calmly reassured the judge that he would see when he read the transcript that Dr. Selikoff had not changed the substance of his direct testimony on the hazards created by drinking Duluth water or breathing Silver Bay air. With that, Edward Fride for Reserve began his cross-examination, a scathing *ad hominem* attack on Dr. Selikoff as a loose-talking publicity-seeker. Judge Lord did question Dr. Selikoff on an issue of substance: if the tissue study originally proposed by him, now being pursued by others, found no amphibole fibers, was the company "home free as far as the health hazard goes?" Dr. Selikoff replied:

> I would think we should find some fibers there. We're looking for needles in a haystack, but that's all right, we should find needles in the haystack with all the difficulties of the study, the technical difficulties, if we examine sufficiently large numbers of samples in some instance we should find some fibers there.

By noon, the cross-examination of Dr. Selikoff was over and he was on his way back to New York.

Dr. Selikoff's credibility with the scientific community and the general public was hurt by the story, repeated by word-of-mouth, of his opening testimony on the morning of September 21 — particularly his withdrawal of his advice to "close your windows." The impression was so widespread in Duluth that Dr. Selikoff had "recanted," that Fayth Glass wrote him about it and sent his return letter, reiterating the warnings of his direct testimony, to the *Duluth News-Tribune*. The week after Dr. Selikoff testified, the general counsel of Armco Steel reported to the company's officers that his "contradictory testimony" had "defused the Government's case," so that "the present likelihood of a shutdown of Reserve is remote." And William J. Williams, Executive Vice President of Republic Steel, still says "Dr. Selikoff's testimony as a whole was pretty effective in Reserve's interest." John Hills insists, "The companies were so bent, so zealous in their own defense, that they construed things in a manner no reasonable person would use. Sure, Dr. Selikoff lessened the emotional charge of his direct testimony when he qualified it, but he didn't change the substance. I'm convinced he only acted out of humanitarian motives. He didn't want people thinking they were automatically condemned to death." Members of the staff at Mt. Sinai say: "If it was just up to Irving, you *know* he'd roll up his windows going through Silver Bay."

With Dr. Selikoff's testimony, the United States government and its fellow plaintiffs concluded the presentation of their public health case to Judge Lord.

• • •

Judge Lord's courtroom was not the only place where the existence of a threat to public health was being weighed. Late in June, Grant Merritt, the Executive Director of the Minnesota Pollution Control Agency, had obtained the approval of Governor Wendell Anderson to meet with Edward Schmid, Reserve's chief public relations officer, and Edward Fride, the company's lead trial attorney. Since the company was already scheduled to shut down first one half of its plant, then the other half, for five weeks during the summer to perform regular maintenance, Merritt asked Schmid and Fride to consider voluntarily closing the entire plant for five weeks, pending resolution of the public health question. The two men had said no. William J. Williams of Republic Steel explains the company's refusal to further curtail production: "This was a period of peak demand for steel. Of course, if we'd thought for a minute there was a serious threat to health . . . ." The records of Armco and Republic Steel reflect only one change in corporate plans as a result of the charge that Reserve Mining was endangering public health — a meeting of Republic Steel's board of directors, scheduled for Silver Bay in the summer of 1973, was shifted to Cleveland in order to avoid public identification of Republic Steel with Reserve. Grant Merritt reflects: "If it were even suggested that an officer of one of the steel companies were putting arsenic in a neighbor's well, I'm pretty sure he'd feel personally responsible. But people in a corporate organization seem to lose that sense of moral responsibility."

At about this time, Mayor Ben Boo of Duluth proposed to his city council that they begin a "crash program" to filter asbestos at the city's water intake. Boo, a maverick Republican, lobbied to gain support for his program among the people he euphemistically calls "the Leadership" of Duluth. The Leadership were already in Reserve's corner. They included Edward Fride, whom Boo calls "a very good friend," the officers of the Northeastern Minnesota Development Association and the Duluth Area Chamber of Commerce, both groups that had voluntarily joined Reserve as defendants when the Federal government filed suit, and Gerald Heaney, once Democratic National Committeeman and a lawyer on behalf of Reserve and other mining interests, by 1973 a judge on the United States Court of Appeals for the Eighth Circuit. (Judge Heaney was still "the gray eminence of the Minnesota Democratic-Farmer-Labor Party" and his advice on the *Reserve* case was sought not only by Mayor Boo, but by Judge Lord and Governor Anderson as well.) The attitude of the Leadership, Boo recalls, was "that the construction of a filtration plant would harm Reserve in court by admitting that there was a health danger." His crash program died, he says, when Judge Heaney refused to swing "his votes" on the city council.

There was little public pressure in Duluth either to construct filtration facilities for the water supply or to stop Reserve's dumping. Some people were buying bottled water in the supermarkets. And, Philip Cook estimates, a thousand or so families regularly filled containers with well water provided for free at Duluth television station WDIO (owned, paradoxically, by Judge Gerald Heaney and associates). But, Donald Mount says, "A common attitude was 'I've been drinking the water for years and I feel fine.'" Mount recalls the reaction when he urged the Duluth school board to provide filtered water for school children. "They wanted to know if my concern was real enough to justify them spending any money." He adds with a resigned smile, "The next item on the agenda was a plan for a new swimming pool." A factor contributing to public indifference about contamination of the water supply was the attitude of the Minnesota Department of Health. From the moment the Minnesota Pollution Control Agency joined the United States in alleging that the Duluth water supply was contaminated, the director of the Department of

Health and his county health officer in Duluth went out of their way to minimize the consequences of such contamination in frequent public statements. The Pollution Control Agency had been created by taking functions from the Department of Health. Judge Lord, himself a veteran of State government, noted that there was "a feud between the Health Department and the State Pollution Control Agency of long standing which might be so intense that it would color the testimony of witnesses on either side."

While the Minnesota Department of Health tried to quiet the concern of Duluth residents, the Federal government did its best to avoid taking any official position beyond the limited warning which it had been cajoled into by the impassioned pleading of Donald Mount and his boss, Stanley Greenfield. At Congressman John Blatnik's request, President Nixon designated Russell Train, the chairman of the Council on Environmental Quality, to coordinate Federal activities related to Duluth's water supply. Theoretically under Train's control, a "Field Operations Center" was established at the National Water Quality Laboratory. The chief scientist at the Field Operations Center was A. Gordon Everett, the senior scientific advisor in EPA's Office of Enforcement. He supervised the collection of hundreds of environmental samples on the Minnesota shore of Lake Superior and the Mesabi Iron Range. One six-man crew spent hours taking air samples in the home of Gary Glass. (An exasperated Fayth Glass told Everett, "This is a goddamned circus.") Because of an error in sampling procedure, the environmental samples could not be analyzed. The sampling program was, a member of Everett's staff concedes, "a disaster." Environmental samples were taken again, distributed to private laboratories, and analyzed over the next several months at a cost to the government of more than $250,000. The results generally confirmed the testimony which William Nicholson gave before Judge Lord in September. The Field Operations Center also assigned an EPA laboratory in Cincinnati to test the effectiveness of various filters in removing amphibole fibers from the Duluth water. A Federal scientist chuckles in retelling a favorite story: laboratory personnel at Cincinnati explained to a visiting professor that containers of water which had passed through various filters were still unanalyzed; they weren't able to evaluate filters because their electron microscope wasn't operational; the professor asked for a flashlight and showed the personnel that many glasses of supposedly filtered water could be discarded immediately — these glasses lit up like Christmas trees as sub-microscopic particles in the water scattered the beam of the flashlight. After observing the Field Operations Center in action, Gary Glass scrounged as many free filters as he could from manufacturers and had them tested. Before the end of 1973, Donald Mount issued a press release without official authorization: Glass' testing had shown that filters made by the Nuclepore company would effectively remove most amphibole fibers when placed on home faucets in Duluth.

In July 1973, Chairman Train visited Duluth, toured the Field Operations Center, flew up the shore of Lake Superior over the Reserve plant, met with Mayor Boo, and held a press conference. Train's visit demonstrated the Federal government's determination to avoid if it possibly could giving the public in Duluth any meaningful advice. Train is a sandy-haired man of medium height and unremarkable appearance, but his voice has the authoritative bass rumble of Smokey the Bear. He says: "My visit was designed to give me on-the-scene familiarity with the problem and show the Federal government's interest. I don't recall any evidence of public concern [and] I didn't want to unintentionally excite public concern."

While the Federal government maintained an inscrutable silence, one arm of the State government, the Department of Health, was publicly minimizing any risk created by Reserve's pollution of the water and air, and another arm, the Pollution Control Agency, was urging strong action based on the same risk. Governor Anderson was reluctant to interfere with the Department of Health. "I didn't feel competent to judge the issue and I didn't have nine months to sort it out," he says. But, an aide notes, Grant Merritt of the Pollution Control Agency "had the ear of the Governor and the Attorney General — and Statewide polls showed that most people supported Grant's position." At Grant Merritt's urging the State of Minnesota filed a motion before Judge Lord in September 1973, requesting a preliminary injunction immediately halting Reserve Mining Company's discharge into Lake Superior and effectively closing the plant. The Save

Lake Superior Association, the Northern Environmental Council and the other environmental groups which had intervened as plaintiffs in the suit had filed a motion for a preliminary injunction at the start of the trial. During the fall, Wisconsin and Michigan added their motions to those of the environmental groups and Minnesota. Judge Lord resisted continued prodding that he rule on these motions for a preliminary injunction. For one thing, he said, electron microscope studies of Duluth tissue were still incomplete. For another, he had warned back in June 1973 that his view of the evidence would depend to some extent on how strongly the Federal government acted upon it, and the Federal government still showed no sign of asking for a preliminary injunction itself.

In July John Hills made the first of many requests to EPA and the Department of Justice for authority to file such a motion on behalf of the United States. Later, he used the motions of the environmental groups and States to argue that the Federal government should move for a preliminary injunction in order to maintain a united front with its co-plaintiffs. Verna Mize supported Hills' argument by tirelessly lobbying her contacts on Congressional staffs; she even obtained a letter from the Republican leader in the House of Representatives, Gerald R. Ford of Michigan, to the Attorney General urging that he "seek an injunction to halt the dumping of taconite tailings into Lake Superior immediately." Michael Gross represented Hills' position at weekly meetings with Alan G. Kirk II, EPA's Acting Assistant Administrator for Enforcement. (Kirk continued in a tenuous "acting" status until he was finally given the permanent Presidential appointment he wanted in December 1973.) "I just wanted Kirk to make a decision one way or the other," Gross recalls. A scientist who attended these meetings recalls Kirk's growing irritation as Gross repeatedly pressed on Hills' behalf for a decision. Kirk says "Hills was just a hired gun. He was supposed to try the case you gave him, whether it was asbestos or tin cans. As the case dragged on, he got too involved in it and lost his objectivity — as you'd expect." Kirk's senior scientific advisor, A. Gordon Everett, says more pointedly, "Hills became a *prima donna* on the issue of a preliminary injunction." The outcome of each meeting with Kirk was always the same: EPA would wait to decide whether to seek a preliminary injunction immediately halting Reserve's discharge, until it had the results of the tissue study proposed by Dr. Selikoff in June. "We were waiting for someone to find the smoking gun," says one EPA official, borrowing a metaphor from Watergate. "It was a mistake."

Hardly anyone at EPA realized that although Dr. Selikoff refused to publicly disown the tissue study, the Mt. Sinai laboratory had quit examining Duluth tissue by electron microscope. Dr. Lawrence Plumlee, who administered EPA's $50,000 research contract with Dr. Selikoff, recalls: "I talked frequently with Bill Nicholson at Mt. Sinai. There was never a clear memo, or even an oral statement, saying they would stop the tissue study. But it appeared by August that the concentration of amphibole fibers in the selected tissues of asbestos workers and Duluth residents was insufficient to get statistically significant results. Counting fibers there was a relevant and noble goal, but almost impossible to achieve. Nicholson and I decided that our research money would be more productively spent on environmental monitoring [examining air and water samples] and the contract was modified accordingly." Dr. Selikoff shrugs off the tissue study, "It seemed like a reasonable approach in June. It was only logical that there must be some tissue burden associated with the gastrointestinal cancers we saw in asbestos workers. But we really hadn't looked quantitatively at workers' tissues outside the lungs." Alan Kirk and his counterparts at the Department of Justice kept delaying a decision on Hills' requests that he be authorized to move for a preliminary injunction, pending the results of a tissue study that Dr. Selikoff would never complete.

●   ●   ●

For the six months following September 1973, Reserve Mining Company presented its case. After reading Reserve's witness list, John Hills stood up to suggest that Judge Lord read Paul Brodeur's then-current series of muckraking articles in the *New Yorker*, exposing the efforts of the asbestos industry to frustrate occupational health regulations. (The series has since been published as a book titled *Expendable Americans*.) As Hills expected, lawyers for Reserve immediately objected that the articles were inadmissible and prejudicial hearsay in a court of law. Hills had no counter argument. Still, he thought, if Judge Lord succumbed to curiosity and secretly read the articles, it couldn't hurt for him to know that Brodeur identified Reserve's leading witnesses as members of a "medical-industrial complex" responsible for hundreds of avoidable cases of disease and death from exposure to asbestos.

But it developed that Hills did not need the Brodeur article to damage the credibility of Reserve's scientific case in Judge Lord's eyes. A consistent approach soon emerged in Reserve's scientific testimony. In designing the Federal government's studies for the *Reserve Mining* case, Gary Glass carefully considered the effects Reserve was most likely to have on Lake Superior; his studies aimed to record those effects, if they existed. Reserve's studies just as carefully aimed to avoid recording likely effects; if the studies inadvertantly created data which showed an effect, then Reserve's scientific consultants either manipulated the data subjectively or, if that was not possible, did not report the data.

It took thousands of hours of preparation and cross-examination to expose this consistent approach. For example, Reserve's first witness attempted to demonstrate that the amphibole mineral cummingtonite-grunerite was entering Lake Superior through tributary streams, using the same x-ray diffraction patterns that had reduced William Phinney, the chief geologist of the manned space-flight program, to helpless laughter. On cross-examination, Hills plodded through the patterns on which the man based his testimony, one at a time.Federal scientists who attended the *Reserve Mining* trial are unanimous in their praise of Judge Lord's insistence that expert witnesses explain the scientific foundations of their opinions, and his quick grasp of the essential points. As Hills' cross-examination wore on, the judge occasionally interrupted, asking the witness to draw two straight lines defining the area of an x-ray diffraction pattern covered by the random squiggles of "background hash," then challenging him to identify a cummingtonite-grunerite peak. The answers he received frequently brought an incredulous smile to his face. The coup-de-grace to Reserve's claim that there were other sources of amphibole fibers in the Lake Superior basin came some weeks later, when another company witness testified that a preliminary examination of samples by low-magnification optical microscope suggested tributary streams were adding amphibole fibers to the lake. On cross-examination, the man acknowledged that a more detailed examination of the same samples had been undertaken by high magnification electron microscope — Reserve had stopped it when examination of the first few samples failed to find a single amphibole fiber.

Hills and the two young Federal attorneys from Washington assisting him frequently worked 12- and 16-hour days through the winter of 1973–1974, to see that every piece of Reserve's evidence was subjected to exhaustive scrutiny. They would meet each morning at the one-room office on the second floor of the Federal courthouse which they shared with a secretary and four other plaintiffs' lawyers — a room stacked to the ceiling with boxes of scientific reports and subpoenaed documents. They generally discussed the day's trial strategy among themselves and with scientific consultants, usually Philip Cook and either William Nicholson or another member of the staff of Mt. Sinai School of Medicine. Meals were generally devoted to skull sessions about the law and science, arguments about tactics and increasingly arcane humor. Many evenings, there was a deposition to be taken from an upcoming Reserve witness at the command post the company's lawyers had established, occupying half a floor atop the tallest and newest skyscraper in downtown Minneapolis. During a recess in a deposition one night, an elderly member of the Mt. Sinai staff looked out a window of the Reserve command post at the Federal courthouse far below. "It makes me think of *The 500 Hats of Bartholemew Cubbins*," he said. "You know — King Derwin stands on the balcony of his castle on the mountain top and looks down at his kingdom. It's a mighty view and it makes him feel mighty important. Then Bartholomew Cubbins stands in the doorway of his family's hut in a cranberry bog and looks up at the King's castle. It's a mighty view, too, but it makes *him* feel mighty small."

Hills spent much of his time keeping other plaintiffs' attorneys informed, making sure he didn't get in the way of anything they wanted to do. And Hills always had time to answer questions from reporters covering the trial about the significance of the day's events. The reporters give Hills high marks: "He was always in control of himself and the situation." "During the whole trial, I never once saw him despondent or nasty." To the extent that the reporters' stories reflected Hills' perceptions of the trial, they contributed to public pressure that Federal and State governments take a strong stand against Reserve. An attorney for the plaintiff environmental groups says, "Hills was a good man to work with. It was clear to me he didn't care whether he ever had another job with the Federal government. His attitude was: I'm the advocate; I'll do what's best to win this case, then send the transcripts to Washington. But out of court he lived with the fear that someone back in Washington would put the lid on his case."

In the courtroom, Hills worried about countering the four major scientific contentions at the core of Reserve's case. The first contention, and the one most easily countered, was that the tailings and airborne dust created by Reserve's operation were not identical to amosite asbestos. Reserve presented leading mineralogists from Harvard University and Manchester University in England to testify that the ore found in the company's Babbitt mine did not look like the variety of cummingtonite-grunerite mined as amosite asbestos. Commercial-grade asbestos was stringier; unlike Reserve's ore, it resembled clusters of horse hairs when examined with the naked eye. Hills did not contest this. Instead, he cross-examined the same experts, using analytical reports and photomicrographs, getting them to admit that much of the finely-crushed particulate matter discharged from Reserve's Silver Bay plant into the air and water was indistinguishable in size, shape, chemistry and crystallographic structure from the dust inhaled and swallowed by amosite asbestos workers. Judge Lord agreed that it was the identical nature of these tiny particles which he should be worried about. If sawdust from pine trees had been shown to cause disease, he said, it would be irrelevant to say you milled stunted pine trees; the relevant question would be whether your sawdust was the same as that shown to cause disease.

Reserve's remaining contentions were presented through the testimony of two of Dr. Selikoff's major antagonists in the occupational health field, Dr. George Wright and Dr. Paul Gross. Dr. Wright was a white-haired, slow-spoken retired clinical physiologist, and a long-time consultant to the Johns Manville Corporation, the country's largest manufacturer of asbestos products. When Edward Fride pressed him to acknowledge Dr. Wright's expertise, Dr. Selikoff would only grant that he was "one of the cleverest physicians I know." Dr. Gross, another elderly consultant to the asbestos industry, was a stocky, goateed man with a heavy German accent. After a distinguished career as a pathologist, Dr. Gross had become a leading experimenter with animals — principally rats. Dr. Selikoff's years of clinical experience with human diseases caused by exposure to asbestos made him disdainful of industry-sponsored animal experiments which purported to show that exposure to asbestos in various circumstances was safe. At meetings, he sometimes taunted Dr. Gross: "What do your furry friends tell you today?"

Reserve's second contention was based on the observations of electron microscopists hired by the company and by the United States that at least 90% of the particles of cummingtonite-grunerite coming from the Reserve plant were very short — less than 5 microns long. Dr. Gross and Dr. Wright both testified that a number of animal experimenters had concluded that commercial asbestos fibers would not produce tumors if they were ground until they were shorter than 5 microns. However, on cross-examination, they acknowledged that other animal experimenters had reached the opposite conclusion, and that there were unresolved scientific questions about the experiments which showed that longer fibers were necessary to cause cancer. They also acknowledged that microscopic examination showed more than 90% of the dust particles in asbestos factories with increased rates of cancer to be shorter than 5 microns. Furthermore, John Hills established that Dr. Wright and Dr. Gross had recently sat with Dr. Selikoff on a scientific committee which considered asbestos pollution. After Dr. Wright and Dr. Gross had been given an opportunity to discuss and comment upon drafts of the committee's report, the committee had unanimously concluded: "there is no body of scientific knowledge which permits the assigning of relative risk factors to fibers less than five microns compared with fibers longer than five microns."

Reserve also contended that people living along the Minnesota shore of Lake Superior were not exposed to as many amphibole particles as were asbestos workers who had increased rates of cancer. This was perhaps the most difficult contention to deal with. William Nicholson had acknowledged in his testimony for the government that his calculations in this regard were necessarily rough. Dr. Wright used two industry-sponsored surveys of workers to argue that there was a threshold, below which exposure to asbestos fibers would not cause cancer of the lung or gastrointestinal tract. Coached by Nicholson and armed with a pocket calculator, John Hills attacked the statistical foundation for Wright's opinion in a mind-numbing, three-day cross-examination on the two studies. Hills became so engrossed in his statistics at one point that Edward Fride objected he wasn't giving Dr. Wright a chance to answer. Hills replied, "I'm perfectly happy to go about my figuring and computations without the witness' interjections, Your Honor." Judge Lord had to remind him that he was in a court of law, bound by the rules of evidence. Finally Dr. Wright admitted to Hills that the first study reported as many excess lung cancer deaths at some "safe" levels of exposure as at "unsafe" levels. This study reported that workers exposed to "safe" levels of asbestos dust had a standard mortality ratio for lung cancer deaths of 167 — in other words, Dr. Wright was accepting as safe a level of exposure which produced two-thirds more lung cancer deaths than in the general population. The conclusions of the second study were based upon cancer death statistics expressed in terms of "equivalent average death rate." As Hills plodded on relentlessly, Dr. Wright wearily admitted: "Well, it is a very peculiar term, equivalent average death rate, and I must confess, sir, that I wish I really understood it well. Before coming here I looked it up and read about it in the statistics books, and I don't think I am good enough to tell you specifically what it means. All I know is that it is used and it is an acceptable way of rating things." Even if these industry studies had established a level of exposure to asbestos that would not cause cancer of the lung or gastrointestinal tract, Dr. Wright and Dr. Gross acknowledged that they were unable to name a threshold level below which exposure to asbestos would cause no mesotheliomas (cancers of the lining of the chest and abdomen), since mesotheliomas had been reported in association with very light exposures (among persons working only a few months with asbestos or merely living in the neighborhood of an asbestos factory).

Reserve's final contention was made by Dr. Gross, who testified that it might be dangerous to breathe asbestos, but he would happily let his grandchildren eat it. Dr. Gross explained that he had fed tailings and amosite asbestos to rats, then dissected the rats and examined their tissues by electron microscope. He announced that his studies showed it was harmless to swallow amphibole particles, since the particles could not penetrate the wall of the gastrointestinal tract. But a detailed search of Dr. Gross' data books suggested that Dr. Gross' study had demonstrated the opposite of what he intended: amphibole particles do indeed penetrate the wall of the gastrointestinal tract. During prolonged cross-examination, Dr. Gross' explanations of seemingly inconsistent data became more and more labored. Ultimately, Judge Lord wrote: "After observing Dr. Gross and listening to his testimony for several days the Court has serious questions as to this witness' ability to report as an unbiased investigator and consequently as to his credibility." A professor of preventive medicine at the University of Wisconsin testified for the plaintiffs that Reserve's argument for the safety of ingesting asbestos had a fatal flaw: "every single report of clinical disease as the result of asbestos exposure includes a substantial number of individuals who have developed cancers in the rectum, the bowel, or the colon, the stomach and the esophagus. And there is no evidence to my knowledge which suggests that these fibers get there any other way to produce cancer than by ingestion."

In January 1974, Reserve Mining Company rested its public health case. On February 5, a stern-voiced Judge Lord announced from the bench that the plaintiffs had "made a *prima facie* case of a public health threat by the discharge into the air and into the water." He went on: "If at the end of this case I am still as concerned about the public health as I am now, I will consider closing the plant immediately . . . the more evidence I hear the closer I come to a conclusion. Reserve has offered nothing that has weakened or rebutted the testimony of the government's experts on the health issue insofar as I, as a finder of fact, am concerned."

John Hills unwound briefly. There was still a lot of work to be done, but after more than four months of nearly constant strain, he had successfully neutralized Reserve's case. He and the other plaintiffs' lawyers had a boisterous party. In the middle of the party, Hills and Grant Merritt telephoned Verna Mize to share the good news. Victory seemed to be in sight.

All of the evidence on public health was not in, however. Back in June of 1973, during the week after John Hills filed Dr. Selikoff's witness statement, lawyers for Reserve complained to Judge Lord that they were having difficulty obtaining a witness of comparable stature: for example, doctors from Minnesota's own Mayo Clinic were unwilling to appear as witnesses for the company, but they might be willing to appear as impartial witnesses hired by the court itself. John Hills voiced some reservations, but Judge Lord agreed to contact the Mayo Clinic. During that first week, Judge Lord's initial, unsure reactions seemed to be those of a politician who wanted to share the responsibility for decision-making. It might be easier for the judge to decide disputed scientific issues if he could rely on the testimony of an impartial court witness. (In much the same way political decision-makers at the Lake Superior Enforcement Conference had relied on Donald Mount as a sort of ultimate expert on disputed scientific issues.) Reserve's lawyers were apparently hoping that the Mayo Clinic witness would be a microbiologist with whom they were already on friendly terms. Instead, the clinic responded to Judge Lord's request by assigning the job to Dr. Arnold L. Brown, chairman of its department of pathology and anatomy. Asbestos was not Dr. Brown's particular area of expertise, but he did have a long-standing interest in the causes of cancer and he had published an article describing a case study of asbestosis by electron microscope. Judge Lord asked Dr. Brown to undertake two main jobs: to arrange for an impartial electron microscope examination of Duluth autopsy tissue parallel to that proposed by Dr. Selikoff, and second, to be present in court to hear the medical testimony on both sides.

Dr. Brown's first action as the court's witness was to attend a meeting at Mt. Sinai School of Medicine in New York, at which Dr. Selikoff gave the details of the tissue study he proposed. The night before the meeting, Dr. Brown recalls, he was summoned to a private dining room at "21" where Reserve's lawyers and scientists "tried to bring me into the picture. One fellow from Armco, I think it was, kept telling me it would be an economic catastrophe if Reserve closed. I felt a little uncomfortable." The next morning Reserve's lawyers whisked him off to Mt. Sinai in a limousine. He shakes his head, "Those guys do travel first cabin." After the meeting at Mt. Sinai, Dr. Brown arranged to have a leading mineralogist at the University of South Wales in Great Britain examine Duluth autopsy tissue for the presence of amphibole fibers.

A genial, handsome man dressed in a conservative, well-tailored sportscoat, his dark hair graying, Dr. Brown would appear in the courtroom whenever medical testimony was given in the *Reserve Mining* case, sitting to Judge Lord's left in the front corner of the jury box. By April 1974, when he received the results of the tissue study which he had arranged at Judge Lord's request, Dr. Brown had been ready for some time to give his medical opinion. The judge had gained considerable self-confidence in evaluating the scientific detail of the case, and it is doubtful that he still wanted Dr. Brown's presence in court. Nevertheless, Judge Lord had hired him as the court's witness and was committed to hear his testimony.

Dr. Brown was preceded to the stand by the mineralogist who had examined Duluth autopsy tissue for him, and by a statistician from the Mayo Clinic. The two men reported that the tissue study was a wash, just as Dr. Selikoff had feared when he quietly abandoned it. There was "no indication of occupational exposure to asbestos dust" in the Duluth tissue and no statistically significant difference between the concentrations of amphibole fibers in the tissues of Duluth residents and those of an unexposed control population. John Hills cross-examined both men. The mineralogist acknowledged that he had only examined lung tissues from asbestos workers, so he had no idea how many fibers might be found in other organs of people occupationally exposed to asbestos. He had once examined sections of stomach wall from six people who had died of peritoneal mesothelioma — diffuse cancer of the lining of the abdomen; asbestos is the only known cause of this cancer, yet he'd found very few asbestos fibers there. In all, the mineralogist testified, his study had included about enough tissue to cover the blunt end of a straight pin, one two-billionth of a man's total body weight, and the significance of the few fibers found in that small amount of tissue had been further obscured by a serious contamination problem. The statistician testified that there were excess concentrations of amphibole fibers in Duluth tissues as compared to control tissues. The excess was in the same range as the limited concentrations of fibers Nicholson of Mt. Sinai testified he had found outside the lungs of asbestos workers. The problem was, the statistician said, the sample was so small that the excess concentration did not satisfy scientists' standard statistical test: that is, it could not be predicted from these results that repeated reexaminations of the same tissues would show an excess concentration 95 out of 100 times.

When Dr. Brown took the stand, he was cross-examined gingerly by Edward Fride and John Hills. First, he dismissed the tissue study, about which he was privately unenthusiastic. Dr. Brown assumed that there were "few, if any" fibers in the tissues of Duluth residents and that "probably we aren't dealing with a time element which is as pressing as it would have been if there had been fibers found in the tissues." But, he said, "I could not conclude from the absence of these fibers that no health hazard exists." Similarly, Dr. Brown testified, the absence of an increase in the Duluth cancer rate attributable to Reserve did not show the absence of a health hazard: "If I were to be concerned about an outbreak of the measles, I wouldn't count the number of cases until after the ten-day incubation period. This is my problem here." Dr. Brown emphasized that amphibole asbestos was very dangerous: it was one of only 15 or 20 substances with a demonstrated record of causing cancer in humans, not just in experimental animals. Dr. Brown dismissed Reserve's attempts to distinguish its ore from commercial-grade amphibole asbestos: the cummingtonite-grunerite discharged by Reserve into the air and water "could not be predicted to act differently than asbestiform fibers which have been implicated in human disease." He also dismissed Reserve's contentions that short fibers do not cause cancer and that asbestos fibers cannot cross the wall of the gastrointestinal tract. But Dr. Brown did not — said that he could not — dismiss Reserve's contention that people living along the Minnesota shore of Lake Superior were not exposed to as many amphibole fibers as were asbestos workers who had increased rates of cancer. The measurement of concentrations of asbestos in environmental samples was too imprecise to permit a definitive scientific conclusion, he said.

Back in the summer of 1973, Judge Lord had told Dr. Brown and Dr. Selikoff that "you scientists" proved everything to the nth degree, but that was not necessary in this case. This was not a criminal case where the government's burden of proof was "beyond a reasonable doubt," he informed them, but a civil case where the burden was "more probable than not" — in other words, the judge was required to decide any disputed issues, not on the basis of the scientists' standard 95% confidence level, but on the basis of a 51% probability. Now, in April 1974, Dr. Brown testified that he did not have adequate evidence to conclude *as a scientist* that there would or would not be increased cancer rates because of the concentrations of amphibole fibers found in the air of Silver Bay or the water of Duluth. He told Judge Lord that "the presence of a known human carcinogen, sir, is in my view cause for concern, and if there are some means of removing that human carcinogen from the environment that should be done." He went on, "*as a physician*, who would rather see well people than sick people . . . my advice to whoever is concerned with this problem is that the people in Duluth, or in Silver Bay, Beaver Bay, or wherever, should not have these fibers present."

The ultimate legal question in the *Reserve Mining* case was whether the company's discharges into the air and water would more probably than not result in irreparable harm, unless they were enjoined. Given the carefully equivocal nature of Dr. Brown's testimony, bristling with qualifications that damaged the cases of both the company and the government, neither Edward Fride nor John Hills felt confident enough of the answer to ask Dr. Brown the ultimate legal question. Judge Lord would have to decide that question for himself.

VII

The Most Favorable Terms Possible

Most legal scholars divide American judges into two broad philosophical camps. The followers of U.S. Supreme Court Justice Oliver Wendell Holmes are said to practice "judicial restraint": these judges protect the dignity and independence of the judiciary by waiting until issues are raised by parties to a lawsuit, by resolving those issues only if they must be resolved in order to decide the case, and even then by resolving the issues as much as possible in accordance with legal precedents. The followers of Justice William O. Douglas are said to be "judicial activists": these judges accept the courts as part of the political process, reach out for troubling issues to resolve, and frankly acknowledge the role of social values in their decisions. As a rule the latter group are political liberals, sharing the faith of the man who appointed Justice Douglas, Franklin D. Roosevelt: "Dante tells us that divine justice weighs the sins of the cold-blooded and the sins of the warm-hearted on different scales."

Miles Lord is a judicial activist. He calls Justice Douglas his model as a judge. His lean features, informality, quick, impatient questioning, and restlessness in court, are reminiscent of Justice Douglas. He also has Justice Douglas' boundless natural energy which separates him, as much as his philosophy, from practitioners of judicial restraint. Once Judge Lord came upon a group of lawyers meeting in a conference room of the Minneapolis Federal courthouse. "Gentlemen," he said, pointing to a door leading from the conference room to the adjoining office of the U.S. Attorney, which he had occupied for six years, "did I ever tell you how that door got there? Well, I tried for months to get GSA [the Federal government's housekeeping agency] to put in a door. Got nothing but red tape. So one weekend I came in with a sledgehammer and busted a hole in the wall about the size of the doorway. Monday, I called up GSA and told them 'When you fix that hole, remember to put a door there.' " Recalling his days as a tough, innovative prosecutor, Judge Lord added reflectively, "You know, if the job had life tenure, I'd still rather be U.S. Attorney."

From the beginning of the trial in *United States of America v. Reserve Mining Company*, Judge Lord was not content just to sit listening to evidence (and even when he was listening to evidence he was often pacing restlessly behind the bench in his stocking feet). During the late summer of 1973, he began searching for some way to halt any pollution coming from Reserve and still keep the plant open. In chambers, he urged the lawyers for the plaintiffs and defendants to explore the possibility of a settlement. The initial reaction of the lawyers was cautious. John Hills said that the United States had brought suit because Reserve's present discharge and the deep pipe were both unacceptable, yet the deep pipe was still the only alternative that Reserve was willing to offer. "If they have already made the decision that they will close down before they go to any form of total on-land disposal," Hills commented, "I am not sure how much there is to talk about." Judge Lord agreed and added, "I would direct that Reserve lay its cards on the table." Robert Sheran for Reserve assured the judge that he was interested in pursuing a settlement, but said that he was "a little uncertain of my authority in the matter . . . . I would feel much more comfortable if Mr. Fride were present." A week passed. In chambers, the attorney for the Save Lake Superior Association and the other plaintiff environmental groups joined Hills in asking Reserve to state its intended course of action "if some sort of on-land disposal might ultimately be ordered by this court." Judge Lord directed, "Let's have an answer to that proposition."

Summer turned to fall, and fall to winter, but there still was no answer to Hills' question. Reserve continued to put forward the deep pipe as its only alternative method of tailings disposal. Robert Sheran left the case to accept a politically startling appointment from Reserve's long-time foe, Governor Wendell Anderson, as Chief Justice of the Minnesota Supreme Court. (In the three years since Sheran had resigned as an associate justice of the court, pleading that he could not support his family on a judge's salary, his firm had been paid more than $950,000 by Reserve Mining Company.) With Sheran gone, Judge Lord was dealing more with Reserve's other senior lawyer, Edward Fride. A flamboyant advocate perhaps better suited to jury trials, Fride approached the judge in a manner that was alternately obsequious and threatening, like the "heavies" played by Wallace Beery in the movies of the 30's. The judge grew short-tempered with him. One day in chambers, Fride said that "asking my client to operate without discharging into Lake Superior is like cutting off a man's legs and asking him to run." Judge Lord snapped, "That's the most disgusting thing I've ever heard."

By the end of 1973, it appeared certain that Reserve would contest the engineering and economic feasibility of any on-land disposal system. The lawyers who shared the plaintiffs' office all knew that EPA's pretrial documents had argued the advantages of having Reserve's parent corporations, Armco Steel and Republic Steel, in court in the event of such a contest. The State of Minnesota now moved that Judge Lord order Armco and Republic into the case as defendants. Edward Fride argued against the motion. It would not make economic and engineering issues easier to resolve, he said, because "We have opened at Reserve Mining Company the books, we have held out the information . . . . I think the information is here." Besides, he noted, the lawsuit had been initiated by the Federal government, not Minnesota, and "the United States now and in the past has never suggested to this Court the necessity for Armco and Republic to be parties."

At the beginning of January 1974, Judge Lord ordered the joinder of Armco and Republic Steel as defendants. He was reluctant, he said, to write a decree in this case that would require the Reserve plant to close. But Reserve itself only passed through profits to its parent corporations and retained no capital to finance pollution abatement. If the judge ordered Reserve to adopt a system of pollution abatement, only Armco and Republic could tell him where the borderline was — where the system would be so expensive that they would close the plant. Judge Lord gave Armco and Republic the necessary permission to take a special interlocutory appeal from his order to the U.S. Court of Appeals for the Eighth Circuit in St. Louis. Even though the judges of the Eighth Circuit were known to be conservative — especially conservative on environmental questions — Judge Lord believed that the advantages of having Armco and Republic in the case were obvious enough to make his decision unassailable. Armco and Republic promptly appealed from the joinder order. Judges Myron H. Bright, Donald R. Ross and William H. Webster of the Eighth Circuit just as promptly directed Judge Lord to set aside his order. Their decision said that "the district court abused its discretion in ordering Armco and Republic to become parties." The presence of Armco and Republic was not necessary to determine whether Reserve created a hazard to public health, the three judges wrote. If the parent corporations were present they might start recalling witnesses in order to do their own cross-examinations. "We express concern that the resolution of the important 'health hazard' issue might be greatly delayed by such joinder." The plaintiffs were still free, the judges said, to move that Armco and Republic be joined as defendants after the public health evidence was complete.

The plaintiffs' lawyers were surprised by this reversal, but not alarmed. The Eighth Circuit's opinion was on a narrow procedural question and Judge Lord was still free to join the parent corporations as defendants at a later stage of the trial. The plaintiffs' lawyers were growing confident that they could win a favorable decision on the merits from Judge Lord, if the parties did not settle the case. The judge was carefully compiling an exhaustive record, and the Eighth Circuit would presumably be reluctant to wade through 20,000 pages of technical evidence in order to reverse a decision on the merits.

In the meantime, Judge Lord was questioning Edward Fride sharply in open court. "Hypothetically," the judge said, "I am going to block the end of that pipe as it goes into Lake Superior . . . hypothetically then the plant will be virtually overflowing with taconite, it will have to stop . . . . If it is your position that there is nothing . . . feasible except the plan . . . to put the pipe in the bottom of the lake, I want to know that . . . . I want to know what the alternatives are. I don't think it is fair to the Court to play a kind of blind man's bluff on matters of this kind." At a later session Judge Lord said of Reserve's property: "There lies an ore body which somebody will mine some day. I would like to know how Reserve would undertake to mine it without dumping into the lake. Now that is a simple proposition." Still later, he said, "I cannot conceive of a situation where management when faced with these alternatives, unknown as they may be, would not have some tentative plans for an alternative method of on-land disposal . . . . I'd like to know what they are." After several days of the judge's questioning, Edward Fride finally gave a formal response. He had a number of points to make before answering Judge Lord's questions. First, he said, "there can be no substantial investment in the continuation of an operation if in fact that operation has a health hazard." Furthermore, under any plan Reserve would need "some assurances that . . . the ground rules won't change." And they would need "an opportunity to continue the operation" while putting the plan into effect. Judge Lord interrupted him: "Please, Mr. Fride, won't you save your argument until the end of the case and make a response to the questions?" Fride then replied, "Now, Your Honor, the question, I think, precisely posed is: does Reserve have a plan . . . an existing plan . . . if the Court were to order that there be no discharge whatsoever, if I understand it, of tailings, water, or a combination thereof to Lake Superior? . . . The answer is, Your Honor, no. Reserve does not have such a plan . . . . We don't know how Reserve could have such a plan." In February 1974, Fride told Judge Lord that the only pollution control plan Reserve had arrived at was "in fact an underwater plan." The deep pipe, he assured the judge, was "a viable alternative."

For two weeks, Fride and Kenneth Haley, Reserve's Vice President for Research and Development, presented in District Court the deep pipe plan which had been rejected as "unacceptable" by the Lake Superior Enforcement Conference three years earlier. The presentation included the same three-dimensional model of the deep pipe that had been displayed at the conference and had made the rounds of Capitol Hill with the officers of Armco and Republic during the summer of 1971. At the conclusion of this presentation, Judge Lord announced that he, too, found the deep pipe plan unacceptable. The field evidence which EPA had gathered during 1972, showed that phenomena in Lake Superior such as upwelling, internal waves and the winter thermocline all operated to distribute suspended particles far deeper than 150 feet — the level at which the deep pipe would discharge tailings. The judge concluded that the plan would do "very little, if anything" to reduce any threat to human health created by Reserve's discharge. In addition, he said, the deep pipe "may actually increase such a threat." The plan would involve the discharge of complex organic chemicals used as flocculating agents. Some of the building blocks of these chemicals were suspected carcinogens. No one claimed to know how the chemicals would behave over long periods of time in Lake Superior; if they broke down, then suspected chemical carcinogens might enter the drinking water of Duluth and other communities along with amphibole fibers from Reserve's tailings. Medical witnesses had testified earlier in the trial that combined exposure to two carcinogens often has a "potentiating effect" — resulting in far worse cancer rates than would be caused by exposure to both of the carcinogens separately.

Judge Lord rejected the deep pipe, but Reserve appeared to reject any conceivable on-land disposal plan. With supporting testimony from Kenneth Haley, Edward Fride introduced into evidence many of the same documents he had introduced at the Lake Superior Enforcement Conference. The documents showed that Reserve could not relocate the fine crushing and separating parts of its beneficiation plant near its mine at Babbitt, Minnesota, for the same reasons the company had decided not to locate its plant there in the first place. There was not enough water there to operate the mill. There was no land suitable for tailings disposal. Even if Reserve could engineer this relocation, the company projected that its capital cost would be prohibitive — $391 million. Later in the trial, the company raised this figure, first to $452 million, then to $574 million. Reserve was claiming that it would be required to expend more than $50 of capital per ton of annual iron pellet production in order to construct new fine crushing and separating facilities. At the same time, however, other steel companies were announcing the construction of entire new taconite beneficiation operations along the Mesabi range on the same scale as Reserve's — including mine development, coarse crushing, fine crushing and separating, pelletizing, and shipping — at a cost of only $28 of capital per ton. Turning from on-land disposal near the mine at Babbitt to on-land disposal near the Silver Bay plant on the shore of Lake Superior, Fride again introduced documents showing that such a plan would be prohibitively expensive — with a capital cost of nearly one-quarter billion dollars. In addition, he elicited testimony from Kenneth Haley that any such plan would have to include some discharge to Lake Superior. In the winter, Reserve added salt to its coarsely crushed ore for the rail haul from Babbitt to Silver Bay, in order to keep the ore from freezing solid. If Reserve tried to recycle all its process water in the winter, levels of dissolved salt would build up and it would become impossible to form the beneficiated taconite into pellets. This would render the entire plant inoperable, Haley testified.

Matters stood at this impasse when one of Judge Lord's law clerks visited the plaintiffs' litigation office. The judge was suspicious, the clerk told John Hills, that Reserve was withholding engineering and economic evidence that might provide a basis for an acceptable settlement. In his chambers, Judge Lord related his suspicions to his clerks in parable form. He told them that when he was a boy in Crosby, Minnesota, he used to idolize a professional wrestler named Louis. One night he went to a neighboring town to see Louis wrestle. Louis' opponent got a leg lock on him, and there was Louis stretched face down, pounding the mat with his palms in agony. At this point the judge illustrated by throwing himself on his carpet and beating it with his open palms. "All of a sudden it came to me," the judge said, "all Louis had to do to break that hold was roll over." The judge rolled over onto his back and got up, brushing himself off. "Boys," he said with a smile, "ever since then I've said 'Never trust the son of a bitch who's pounding the mat.' " Judge Lord suspected that Reserve's arguments against on-land disposal were so much mat-pounding. And he had an idea how his suspicions could be tested: Hills should subpoena the economic and engineering records of Armco Steel and Republic Steel. Hills was unenthusiastic about this suggestion. During pretrial discovery proceedings, the Government had served extensive written interrogatories on Edward Fride asking Reserve to list every study it had prepared, or was having prepared, concerning the modernization of its plant and alternative methods of disposing of tailings. Fride had returned detailed answers signed under oath, as the law required, by a Reserve officer, Kenneth Haley. Reserve had also agreed to the entry of a pretrial order by Judge Lord requiring both sides to answer interrogatories completely. At a later stage of pretrial discovery, Hills had served Fride with a subpoena commanding that Haley produce every existing document concerning alternative methods of tailings disposal. Hills and his technical advisor, Philip Cook, had spent days checking each document that Haley produced. Hills' cynicism did not extend to the belief that Reserve's officers and lawyers had risked a possible criminal prosecution for perjury and contempt of court by concealing evidence. Still, he decided that it would be better to subpoena the records of Armco and Republic than to risk alienating Judge Lord by rejecting his suggestion.

Three officers of Armco Steel and Republic Steel appeared in Judge Lord's courtroom on March 1, 1974, in response to John Hills' subpoenas. Each was represented by a separately-retained Minnesota lawyer and each brought with him hundreds of documents. Lawyers at the plaintiffs' counsel table hurriedly scanned documents they had never seen before, handing relevant ones to Hills as he questioned the executives.

In a low, even tone, Hills asked the officers of Reserve's parent corporations about the company's claim that it was not feasible to engineer a new concentrator facility and tailings impoundment near its mine at Babbitt. Reserve had introduced as an exhibit, before the Lake Superior Enforcement Conference and before Judge Lord, a document claiming that the company had decided not to locate at Babbitt because there was insufficient water to operate the process and no land for tailings disposal. Now Hills had Republic Steel's Director of Engineering identify a critique of that exhibit prepared by a senior project engineer at

Republic, which said "Many of the statements made here are untrue . . . . The Babbitt site was dropped very early in the game (about 1945) in favor of a site on the shore of Lake Superior. The reasons for moving were economics rather than technical. If a nearly closed system is technically feasible (Erie Mining Co. is operating in this manner), sufficient makeup water is available in the area. Layouts were made . . . showing two different areas suitable for tailings disposal. The Babbitt site must be considered technically feasible."

Documents were piling up at Hills' side. Reporters and television artists were slipping in through a side door to fill the jury box. Hills used another document to investigate Reserve's deep pipe disposal plan. He asked Armco's Vice President for Engineering to identify a two year-old report entitled "Final Recommendation of the Engineering Task Force." The report concluded that "total on-land disposal appears to be the only reasonable method" of both improving Reserve's product (this would require the addition of a toxic chemical to the separation process to float off impurities) and satisfying regulatory agencies. The report stated that recent work had raised "serious questions about the technical and economic feasibility" of the deep pipe concept. The report concluded that "the Engineering Task Force does not recommend pursuing this concept any further." The members of this task force had included the chief engineering officers of Armco, Republic and Reserve; Edward Fride and Kenneth Haley had both attended its meetings.

Judge Lord was visibly angered by the report. He asked Armco's Vice President for Engineering if he realized that the judge had wasted his time "considering a plan . . . which your company put forward as something that was feasible and possible and that they wanted to do, and that you had rejected it in 1972?" Looking back, both C. William Verity, Chairman of the Board of Armco, and William J. Williams, Executive Vice President of Republic, minimize the importance of this task force report. Verity says "the Court said they found in our files an engineering study by Republic or Armco — I don't know — that they felt that was not a feasible route. That was one engineering study out of many. I think all of us felt that was not only a feasible route, but

149

the soundest route." However, these disclaimers are contradicted by the sworn testimony of the chief engineering officers of both Armco and Republic. An angry Judge Lord cross-examined both men closely on March 1. Armco's Vice President for Engineering identified a recent report from a member of his own staff that the deep pipe was not feasible because of pipe replacement problems. The vice president testified that he "would be prepared to take" his staff's recommendation and he did not anticipate he would be overruled. Similarly, Republic's Director of Engineering identified a later report from a member of *his* staff that the deep pipe "as presented to the government is not practical and requires a considerable amount of experimenting and engineering." The director explained, "When it was originally brought out, it was felt that it was a feasible plan . . . . Then, as time went by, it looked like we were not going to be able to put it under water." Judge Lord broke in: had Kenneth Haley of Reserve presented him a plan "which you had concluded was technically infeasible?" The director replied, "Right."

John Hills explored the question of whether Reserve could dispose of its tailings on land near Silver Bay. The engineering task force had dismissed every alternative disposal plan except for one under which Reserve would dispose of all its tailings on land near its Silver Bay plant, at a location called Palisade Creek. No one in the Federal or State governments knew of the existence of this plan; yet hundreds of previously undisclosed documents on Reserve's stationery explored the engineering and economic feasibility of the plan. Reserve's president later testified that his company's engineering department probably devoted 200 times more effort to this Palisade Creek plan than to any other disposal plan after the report of the engineering task force. Reserve's parents had made internal estimates that the capital cost of the plan would be $89 million — rather than the quarter-billion-dollar figure represented to Judge Lord as the minimum cost of on-land disposal. Because the plan would allow Reserve to add flotation reagents to remove impurities from its pellets, it would actually *increase* slightly the amount of profits Armco and Republic realized from the company's operations (by nearly $4 million per year), although not enough to satisfy the corporations' normal rate-of-return standards for making major capital investments. Armco's Vice President for Engineering testified that only the salt added to Reserve's ore during the winter stood between the Palisade Creek plan and a recirculating, zero-discharge system.

That night the evening news in Minneapolis reported the discovery of a "massive corporate coverup."

On March 2, 1974, after the conclusion of the hearing on John Hills' subpoenas, attorneys for Reserve, Armco and Republic informed Judge Lord in his chambers that they were ready to negotiate a settlement. Even before John Hills had drafted his subpoenas, C. William Verity, Chairman of the Board of Armco Steel, had reported to his fellow directors that he still did "not believe the plant will be closed, but plans for on-land disposal will have to be negotiated with the government on the most favorable terms possible." On March 4, Reserve and its parent corporations opened their campaign for the most favorable on-land disposal terms possible by offering the plaintiffs the Palisade Creek plan. The companies announced they had decided that day that they could operate it as a recirculating, zero-discharge system, after all. Their engineers had discovered that they could eliminate the problem of dissolved salt building up in their process water during the winter months, by adding soda ash to precipitate the salt from solution. (Four years later, this was still being hailed as "a technological breakthrough" by Reserve. "Hell," says one of Judge Lord's law clerks, "that's the first experiment we did in introductory chemistry." In 1972, a group of mining engineers from Bethlehem Steel had published a detailed article in the *Transactions of the American Society of Mining Engineers*, explaining that salt was often added to taconite ore to prevent freezing, but that dissolved salt in the process water was detrimental to forming strong iron pellets. The article went on to state that work at Bethlehem had showed the addition of soda ash "should result in the essentially complete precipitation" of dissolved salt from the process water.)

The end of the *Reserve Mining* case seemed close at hand. The plaintiffs to the suit selected a negotiating team chaired by a junior EPA lawyer who had been helping John Hills. The team included Donald Mount, the Director of EPA's National Water

151

Quality Laboratory, Grant Merritt, the Executive Director of the Minnesota Pollution Control Agency, and representatives of the Minnesota Department of Natural Resources, other State governments and environmental groups. Before they began negotiating with Reserve, the plaintiffs met by themselves to thresh out a number of important issues. For example, how much turn-around time should Reserve have to abate its discharges to the air and water? Estimates ranged from 18 to 36 months. More basically, where should Reserve be allowed to dispose of its tailings? All of the plaintiffs thought a tailings impoundment near Reserve's mine at Babbitt would harm the environment much less than one near the Silver Bay plant. Mining engineers from the Minnesota Department of Natural Resources took essentially the same position they'd taken at meetings of the Lake Superior Enforcement Conference Technical Committee: they were unwilling to approve a disposal site near Silver Bay until Reserve, Armco and Republic showed that they had made a good faith effort to solve the problems at Babbitt. But the members of the plaintiffs' negotiating team agreed that such issues should take a back seat to achieving agreement in principle on protecting public health. To ensure that matters in Minneapolis did not get out of hand, Alan Kirk, EPA's Assistant Administrator for Enforcement, asked Pamela Quinn, a lawyer in his office, to go there and report developments in the negotiations directly to him. Quinn called the EPA lawyer who was helping Hills — he was a fellow veteran of the agency's old litigation office — and said, "I figure I'd better take the job or you might get a real spy." Quinn's primary loyalty to the trial team in Minneapolis, rather than her superiors in Washington, was reinforced when she began dating John Hills shortly after her arrival in Minneapolis. (She married him after the trial.) Her "reports" to Kirk were innocuous and the plaintiffs' negotiating team set about its business much as John Hills had conducted the trial — substantially without any policy guidance or supervision from Washington.

At their first negotiating session with Reserve, Armco and Republic, the plaintiffs' negotiating team began by pointing out that Judge Lord had ruled there was a *prima facie* case Reserve's discharges to the water and air created a hazard to public health.

Unless there was some startling new evidence, they expected Judge Lord would stand by this ruling in any final decision. Therefore, they insisted that Reserve use the best available technology to prevent the discharge of amphibole fibers into the water and air. The plaintiffs interpreted best available technology to mean no discharge to the water and the installation of filtering devices on Reserve's exhausts to the air in accordance with Minnesota Air Pollution Control Regulation 17. The defendants' team, led by Edward Fride, brushed aside the plaintiffs' reliance on Judge Lord. He'd already been reversed once by the Eighth Circuit, they said. They were offering the Palisade Creek plan, essentially as discovered in the files of Armco and Republic. There would be no discharge of amphibole fibers into the water, but use of the best available technology on discharges to the air was out of the question — it would be too expensive. In addition, their offer of the Palisade Creek plan was subject to a number of important (and, to the plaintiffs, unpalatable) conditions. Neither side budged significantly from its opening position — for the plaintiffs, tailings disposal with maximum environmental controls, preferably within two years and near Reserve's mine at Babbitt; for the defendants, tailings disposal with lesser controls after five years near Reserve's plant at Silver Bay, and subject to preconditions. It was apparent by late March that the negotiations were going nowhere. At that time Russell Train, who'd been shifted from the President's Council on Environmental Quality to become the Administrator of EPA, called a staff meeting to consider once again whether EPA should seek a preliminary injunction immediately halting Reserve's discharges to the water and air. His Deputy Administrator, John Quarles, expressed his usual reservations about precipitous action. "There are lots of threats to public health," he explains, "and it's probably socially unwise — in any event politically impossible — to stop every plant that presents a threat to public health." Train doesn't recall any political pressure from the White House in support of Quarles' position. By now the White House was virtually paralyzed by Watergate and the increasing likelihood of impeachment. Anyway, Train says, "John Quarles was probably much more sensitive to this aspect of the problem than I was." Quarles was giving Train the same counsel of political caution that he'd given Acting Administrator Fri the previous year, but Assistant Administrator for Enforcement Alan Kirk no longer advised delay. Earlier in the day, Kirk had been visited by Verna Mize. "A lot of these people are kooks," Kirk says, "but she wasn't a kook, she was rational. She said flat out, 'You people have looked long enough!' " Kirk's two principal deputies were also pushing him to seek a preliminary injunction. William Nicholson had demonstrated electron microscope procedures to one of the deputies at the Mt. Sinai School of Medicine in the summer of 1973. The deputy had immediately thought how difficult Dr. Selikoff's proposed tissue study was, and how overly optimistic people were about what the study could show. In February 1974, the deputy had finally taken the extraordinary step of bypassing Kirk's scientific advisor, Gordon Everett, and reading some trial transcripts for himself — especially Dr. Selikoff's testimony — and he had been impressed by the seriousness of the hazard to public health. Pressures from Mrs. Mize and his own staff seem to have affected Kirk's decision in favor of a preliminary injunction. "I didn't think the evidence was that clear either way," he says. "The decision was almost metaphysical. You know — how will the decision be perceived, by the public, by agency personnel (that affects morale), by industry (that affects our clean-up program), by the White House?" At the end of his staff meeting, Russell Train sided with Kirk. He would ask the Department of Justice to seek a preliminary injunction against Reserve. Train's analysis of his decision, like Kirk's, is unrelated to the particulars of the evidence. Train had only met Dr. Selikoff a couple of times and had formed no opinion as to his reliability, he says, even though "there really wasn't anyone else" to look to for expert advice. In the end, Train says, "I was increasingly concerned . . . . The Agency was charged with protecting the environment and the public. People just wouldn't understand it if we stood by any longer."

Near the end of March, the plaintiffs' negotiating team revealed to Reserve, Armco and Republic that John Hills had been authorized to file a motion for a preliminary injunction against Reserve on behalf of the United States. That afternoon, the Minnesota lawyers for Armco and Republic agreed to recommend to their clients in Ohio that they accept the plaintiffs' basic demand for the use of the best available technology to prevent the discharge of amphibole fibers into the water and air. At the end of the day, the Armco and Republic lawyers were able to counter the impact of the Federal government's motion by informing Judge Lord that some progress was finally being made toward settlement. Briefly, the plaintiffs' team shifted its attention to internal meetings to decide what counter-concessions to offer the companies on other issues. These internal meetings were still going on when Armco and Republic rejected the advice of their Minnesota lawyers and refused once more to adopt the best available air pollution control technology. By mid-April, the plaintiffs' negotiating team announced in open court that settlement negotiations were, for all practical purposes, dead.

It was now Judge Lord's turn to act. Following the completion of testimony by the court's medical witness, Dr. Brown, Judge Lord ordered the chief executive officers of Armco Steel and Republic Steel to appear in his courtroom. The legal basis for this order was that he had once again joined Armco and Republic as defendants to the lawsuit, and the plaintiffs wanted to make a record this time that would convince the Eighth Circuit that the joinder was proper. The chief executive officers were, in fact, questioned for three days on matters related to joinder by lawyers for the States of Minnesota and Wisconsin. While they were on the stand, Judge Lord asked a number of questions which had a different aim, however. He was trying to wring from the officers concessions which the plaintiffs' negotiating team had been unable to win.

The senior corporate executive in Judge Lord's courtroom during these three days was C. William Verity, Chairman of the Boards of Armco Steel Corporation and of Reserve Mining Company. Like Judge Lord, Verity was born and had grown up in a steel company town. But his family were not unemployed miners in Crosby, Minnesota. His grandfather, George M. Verity, founded the American Rolling Mill Company of Middletown, Ohio. Today, a life-size bronze statute of George Verity stands outside the window of his grandson's office at Armco's corporate headquarters in Middletown.

Like Judge Lord, Verity had long been active in politics. But he was certainly not a populist Statehouse politician. Rather, Verity was an influential national figure in the Republican party who dined at the White House and met frequently with cabinet members when the Republicans were in power.

Both Verity and Judge Lord are concerned about the future of their country. Judge Lord finds support for his views in E.F. Schumacher's *Small Is Beautiful*. Schumacher says that the industrial age considers "money to be all-powerful": "the development of production and the acquisition of wealth have become the highest goals of the modern world in relation to which all other goals, no matter how much lip service may still be paid to them, have come to take second place." The result, Schumacher argues, is "a system of production that ravishes nature and a type of society that mutilates man." Today physical events such as pollution and resource exhaustion are fulfilling the function of ancient sages and teachers "to challenge materialism and plead for a different order of priorities." Schumacher does not ask that our industrial system be dismantled, but he does urge that we undertake "the reconciliation of opposites which, in strict logic, are irreconcilable": a society organized by the market system and economic self-interest must learn to take into account the Judeo-Christian ideals expressed in the Bible — humility in the presence of the natural world ("The Lord . . . made the Pleiades and Orion, and turns deep darkness into the morning and darkens the day into night, . . . calls for the waters of the sea, and pours them out upon the earth . . . . Lo, these are but the outskirts of his ways; and how small a whisper do we hear of him!") and the subordination of material wealth to higher values ("Do not lay up for yourselves treasures on earth where moth and rust consume and where thieves break in and steal . . . . Is not life more than food, and the body more than clothing?")

Discussing what's wrong with America, Verity cites Ayn Rand's *Atlas Shrugged*. In contrast to Schumacher, Rand says, "To the glory of mankind, there was, for the first and only time in history, a country of money — and I have no higher, more reverent tribute to pay to America, for this means: a country of reason, justice, freedom, production, achievement." She argues that "his own happiness is man's only moral purpose," and vigorously attacks thirty centuries of Judeo-Christian ethics as a doctrine of "hatred-eaten mystic parasites" — a doctrine which threatens to erode the pride and the "radiant selfishness of soul" on which the achievements of the industrial age are based. Rand warns, "There are two sides to every issue: one side is right and the other is wrong, but the middle is always evil . . . . In that transfusion of blood which drains the good to feed the evil, the compromiser is the transmitting rubber tube."

A small, distinguished-looking man with white hair and black eyebrows, Verity chooses his words carefully. It was, he says, "a shocking experience" for him to sit on the witness stand and watch the way Judge Lord handled the *Reserve Mining* case. A reporter who covered the trial observes that Judge Lord became "increasingly hostile" toward Reserve, Armco and Republic over the course of the nine-month trial. William J. Williams of Republic Steel agrees on reflection that the judge "probably did become more hostile as the case went on." On the other hand, Verity, interviewed several years after the *Reserve Mining* trial, does not try to conceal his contempt (in the everyday, rather than the legal, sense of the word) for Judge Lord. In the course of the interview, Verity identified the other men who have tried Armco pollution cases by their courtesy titles (for example, "Judge Hannay" and "Judge Eckman") while referring to Judge Lord repeatedly and exclusively as "Mr. Lord" — as though he had found Miles Lord unfit and impeached him in his mind. "Mr. Verity was always courteous," recalls John Hills, "but I got the clear impression he was a powerful man and he knew it — he wasn't about to take orders from a U.S. District Judge."

Verity's third day on the witness stand was Saturday, April 20, 1974. Late Saturday morning, Judge Lord lectured him from the bench: "I have stated fairly consistently that I would do everything I could to prevent the closing of the plant." He recalled that he had tried to promote a negotiated settlement at the beginning of the trial by asking if Reserve "could bring any sort of skeleton plan forward which would provide for on-land disposal." Edward Fride had objected that his inquiry prejudged the case, that Reserve wanted him to consider the deep pipe plan. He had waited six months and had heard the deep pipe plan, the judge told Verity. "I myself decided it was a joke . . . just another presentation by Armco and Republic to delay . . . the inevitable day when that discharge would be taken out of the lake . . . . That's six months later and ten million dollars profit later and fifty billion fibers later down the throats of the children in Duluth." More months had passed since he had rejected the deep pipe. Now, he said, he was "faced with the prospect of a stranded population, hostages of the Reserve Mining Company, . . . because Armco and Republic have seen fit to hold out for the last dollar of profit and to the last point of time . . . . Your own internal documents indicate the game you've been playing with the Court. At what point, Mr. Verity, do you think you can stop this kind of thing?" The judge said he would give Verity and the president of Republic Steel the lunch hour to decide "whether you can meet the requirements that there be complete on-land disposal . . . the requirements of Air Pollution Control Regulation No. 17 . . . and the requirements of the State Department of Natural Resources."

After lunch, Verity returned to the stand and read: "I as Chairman of the Board of Reserve Mining Company make the following statement . . . . It is our considered judgment that Reserve's discharges do not constitute a health hazard and they are not in violation of the State and Federal permits granted to Reserve." Since Reserve and its parent corporations wanted to continue operations, they were nevertheless prepared "with no concession of liability" to begin engineering immediately on the Palisade Creek on-land disposal plan with a zero-discharge, recirculating water system. However, the companies were not prepared to meet Air Pollution Control Regulation No. 17. Finally, Verity read, "Integral parts of this offer are the following conditions":

(1) Reserve would continue operating for the five years during which the on-land disposal system would be built.

(2) The Court would see to it that State and Federal agencies issued permits insuring that Reserve's operation under

the Palisade Creek plan would be permitted to continue without further interruption until the company's ore body was exhausted.

(3) The Court would make "a satisfactory resolution of the alleged health hazard issues," so that the project would be attractive to investors.

(4) State and Federal governments would extend such "financial assistance as may be legally available, including assistance with industrial revenue bonds."

A veteran political reporter says "Verity's reading of that statement was the most amazing display of arrogance I've ever seen. I'm no fan of Miles Lord, but it was like Armco and Republic were giving him the finger right in his face." Judge Lord, grim-faced, asked a few clarifying questions and remained behind the bench for the afternoon of April 20, hearing more testimony from the two chief executive officers. During a recess, he called his two law clerks to his chambers. They had already prepared all of his opinion in *United States of America* v. *Reserve Mining Company* except for the relief he was to order. The judge and his clerks hurriedly finished the opinion. Behind the bench again, Judge Lord announced that he was ready to deliver his opinion. First, he read his terse findings of fact:

> Reserve Mining Company (Reserve) is set up and run for the sole benefit of its owners, Armco Steel Corporation (Armco) and Republic Steel Corporation (Republic), and acts as a mere instrumentality or agent of its parent corporations. Reserve is run in such a manner as to pass all its profits to the parents.
>
> Reserve acting as an instrumentality and agent for Armco and Republic discharges large amounts of minute amphibole fibers into Lake Superior and into the air of Silver Bay daily.
>
> The particles when deposited into the water are dispersed throughout Lake Superior and . . . . are found in substantial quantities in the Duluth drinking water.

159

Many of these fibers are morphologically and chemically identical to amosite asbestos and an even larger number are similar to amosite asbestos.

Exposure to these fibers can produce asbestosis, mesothelioma, and cancer of the lung, gastrointestinal tract and larynx . . . .

While there is a dose-response relationship associated with the adverse effects of asbestos exposure and may be therefore a threshold exposure value below which no increase in cancer would be found, this exposure threshold is not now known . . . .

Most of the studies dealing with this problem are concerned with the inhalation of fibers; however, the available evidence indicates that the fibers pose a risk when ingested as well as when inhaled . . . .

The discharge into the air substantially endangers the health of the people of Silver Bay and surrounding communities as far away as the eastern shore in Wisconsin.

The discharge into the water substantially endangers the health of the people who procure their drinking water from the western arm of Lake Superior including the communities of Beaver Bay, Two Harbors, Cloquet, Duluth, and Superior, Wisconsin.

He then read his conclusions of law, stating that Reserve's discharges into the air and into Lake Superior were subject to abatement under Federal statutes, State regulations, and the common law of nuisance. Finally, the judge read the memorandum supporting his findings and conclusions. In the memorandum, he rejected Verity's offer of the Palisade Creek plan, which did not "effectively deal with the problem caused by the discharge of amphibole fibers into the air." He also rejected each of the conditions that Verity had attached to the plan. The threat to public health made five years of continued discharge unacceptable. The judge doubted that he had the authority to immunize Reserve's operations from future environmental regulations. Compensation from Federal and State governments was unnecessary. Judge Lord's memorandum concluded:

> Finally, the proposal was conditioned upon favorable findings by the Court as to the public health issues. The Court finds this condition to be shocking and unbecoming in a court of law. To suggest that this or any other court would make a finding of fact without regard to the weight of the evidence is to ask that judge to violate the oath of his office and to disregard the responsibility that he has not only to the people but also to himself . . . .
>
> Up until the time of writing this opinion the Court has sought to exhaust every possibility in an effort to find a solution that would alleviate the health threat without a disruption of operations at Silver Bay. Faced with the defendants' intransigence, even in the light of the public health problem, the Court must order an immediate curtailment of the discharge.
>
> Therefore it is ordered:
>
> 1) That the discharge from the Reserve Mining Company into Lake Superior be enjoined as of 12:01 A.M., April 21, 1974.
>
> 2) That the discharge of amphibole fibers from the Reserve Mining Company into the air be enjoined as of 12:01 A.M., April 21, 1974 until such time as defendants prove to the Court that they are in compliance with all applicable Minnesota Regulations including but not limited to APC 17.

On Sunday, April 21, there were no waterfalls of opaque gray water crashing from chutes of the E.W. Davis Works of Reserve Mining Company, flowing over its tailings delta into Lake Superior. No dust was coming from the exhaust stacks of the Reserve plant. The machinery that produced 12% of America's iron was silent. And the three thousand employees of Reserve were out of work.

VIII

Doing The Craven Crawl

On Monday April 22, 1974, Judge Miles Lord was again behind the bench at the Minneapolis Federal courthouse, presiding over a post-trial hearing in the case of *United States of America* v. *Reserve Mining Company*. Judge Lord had ordered the chief executive officers of Armco Steel and Republic Steel to remain in town for this session. Now, he told the two men, "the Court finds itself on the same side as you are, that is . . . this Court will take every reasonable step within its power to help you to reopen that plant." It was evident from the opinion Judge Lord had delivered two days earlier that he was seeking a commitment to an acceptable pollution abatement plan as his price for reopening the Reserve plant. The only response of Reserve, Armco and Republic was to ask that Judge Lord stay his order — allowing them to reopen the plant immediately. The judge denied this motion, and the lawyers for the companies noted that they would apply to the U.S. Court of Appeals for the Eighth Circuit for a stay. Reserve's lead counsel did not appear for more than an hour, so Judge Lord asked where Mr. Fride was. Fride's associate said that he was preparing to meet with a panel of Eighth Circuit judges who were attending a criminal law conference in Springfield.

The plantiffs' lawyers began a head-long race to catch up with Fride. Grant Merritt, the Executive Director of the Minnesota Pollution Control Agency, rushed to a telephone to charter a private plane. In his hurry to take up the chase, he forgot to ask whether Fride was headed for Springfield, Illinois or Springfield, Missouri. He soon found it was the latter. That afternoon Merritt and John Hills, the chief lawyer for the Federal government, accompanied by three lawyers for other plaintiffs and a local reporter, boarded a Learjet at a small St. Paul airfield. As the plane flew south above the valley of the Mississippi River, John Hills had time to think back to his previous trial victory over Armco Steel on the Houston Ship Channel, and how that victory had merely been the beginning point for backstairs political deals. He had time to think even further back to his first big case in Memphis, when he shuttled back and forth between courts in the face of political hostility, only to learn that he had proved his case without any effect at all. Grant Merritt's mind went back to the struggles of his ancestors. After Alfred Merritt and his brothers discovered and began to develop the Mesabi Iron Range, they lost everything they owned to the financial sleight-of-hand of John D. Rockefeller and the founders of U.S. Steel. Alfred Merritt had sued Rockefeller for fraud and misrepresentation, and doggedly pursued his suit despite his reduced circumstances — he had to walk to the trial each day, because he couldn't afford the trolley fare. The U.S. District Court for Minnesota awarded Alfred Merritt a judgment for $940,000. Rockefeller appealed to the Eighth Circuit, which reversed the judgment and ordered a new trial. Penniless, unable to afford a second trial, Alfred Merritt and his family were forced to settle for half of his original judgment. To their bitter resentment, Rockefeller also required them to sign a complete retraction of their charges as the price of settlement. Now their descendant was going before the Eighth Circuit with the risk of losing another hard-won victory over the steel industry.

The plaintiffs' lawyers went directly from the Springfield, Missouri airport to the Drury Inn motel, where the judges of the Eighth Circuit were staying. The judges said they would hear Reserve's motion to stay Judge Lord's order later in the evening, after attending to the business of their criminal law conference. Grant Merritt passed some of the time with a Springfield newspaper. He was immediately struck by a front-page picture of Reserve workers lining up to apply for unemployment benefits in Silver Bay. Merritt recalls that the media had been full of picturesque economic hardship in Silver Bay since Saturday, with very little mention of the invisible threat to public health. Waiting at the motel, the plaintiffs' lawyers came across a man who had fallen on a flight of stairs and injured himself. They offered him help until an ambulance arrived. John Hills, an instinctive plaintiff's lawyer, saw a slippery spot on the stairs where the man had fallen. He had a press photographer take some pictures of the stairs for the injured man, in case he ever wanted to file a personal injury claim against the motel. Merritt recalls Donald R. Ross, one of the Eighth Circuit judges, coming upon this scene and sizing it up with evident distaste.

The hearing on Reserve's motion took place in a room of the Drury Inn. There were card tables for the lawyers and a dinner table covered with a green cloth for the three judges, who filed in wearing business suits. A reporter who was present says, "It had all the earmarks of an impromptu board meeting of your American Legion post." The judges were the same three men who had reversed Judge Lord's order joining Armco and Republic to the lawsuit as defendants. The backgrounds of the three men were remarkably similar. Each was in his early fifties. Before being appointed to the Federal bench, each had practiced corporate law in the major city of his state, with a firm representing banks, utilities, and local industry. None had run for major elective office, but each had been active in his party organization, in those unpublicized areas where, as a contemporary leader has noted, "money is the mother's milk of politics."

The youngest of the judges sat on the right: William H. Webster was a wealthy native of St. Louis who had been appointed to the Federal bench by President Nixon. His handsome, somewhat patrician face displayed no emotion and he rarely spoke. In the center was Myron H. Bright of Fargo, North Dakota, an appointee of President Johnson. His open, friendly face occasionally registered bewilderment at the complexities of the *Reserve Mining* case. To the left sat the most outspoken and articulate of the three judges, Donald R. Ross. His jowly face shadowed by a heavy beard, Judge Ross was often abrupt and rough behind the bench. He was only 30 years old when President Eisenhower appointed him United States Attorney for Nebraska. Four years later, he became embroiled in a scandal over a friend's apparent attempt to bribe members of the U.S. Senate on behalf of the natural gas industry. Ross testified tearfully to a Senate investigating committee that "I have never taken a nickel from anybody since I have been United States Attorney." He resigned his post, he told the committee, after the Attorney General told him he had done "nothing dishonest," but that his actions "might reflect unfavorably on the Department of Justice." After resigning, Ross served as Republican National Committeeman from Nebraska for 13 years. After Barry Goldwater's overwhelming defeat in 1964, he was instrumental in promoting to the chairmanship of the National Committee Ray C. Bliss, then the head of an Ohio Republican Party dominated by companies such as Armco and Republic Steel. He helped Bliss to rebuild a pragmatically conservative party which nominated the pragmatically conservative Richard Nixon for President in 1968. After Nixon was elected, he appointed Donald Ross to the first vacancy on the Eighth Circuit bench.

The judges alarmed Grant Merritt at the opening of the hearing on Reserve's motion for a stay by asking if anyone there opposed the motion, and calling on John Hills; the normal procedure in a court of law is that a party who has made a motion must first convince the court there is some reason to take the action he has requested. Hills argued on the basis of Judge Lord's findings that Reserve's discharges to the air and water "threatened the lives" of people who lived along the Minnesota shore of Lake Superior. Judge Ross questioned Hills sharply. "Show me one individual that's being harmed by this. Show me one dead body," he demanded. At some points, a reporter recalls, Judge Ross seemed openly contemptuous of Judge Lord's rulings. Hills told Judge Ross he couldn't produce hard evidence of past harm, but "Society can't afford to gamble I'm wrong." Edward Fride argued in favor of Reserve's motion: "Quite soon, you're going to have a ripple effect that's going to have a significant effect on the whole economy of the United States."

After less than half-an-hour of arguments, Judge Bright announced that he and his colleagues needed 15 minutes to deliberate. They withdrew to another room. A Minnesota reporter patted Grant Merritt on the shoulder and told him he was sorry he'd lost. The reporter then set his typewriter on the judges' table and wrote the story of their decision, so that he could phone it in the minute it was announced. The judges returned with the expected announcement: they were immediately staying Judge Lord's order. They would hold a more formal hearing in St. Louis next month. In the meantime, Reserve's plant was free to resume operations. Armco and Republic Steel were no longer under any short-term pressure to propose an environmentally acceptable plan to abate the plant's discharges into the air and water.

On May 15, the Eighth Circuit met at the St. Louis Federal courthouse to hear further arguments on their stay of Judge Lord's order. Judge Ross once again led the three judges in questioning John Hills sharply on public health evidence. However, the judges also expressed interest in a new subject at this hearing: those people living along the Minnesota shore of Lake Superior who were concerned about the contamination of their water supply could now bring home filtered drinking water if they wished to make the effort. On April 18, two days before he had ordered the Reserve plant closed, Judge Lord had dusted off a contingency plan to provide temporary supplies of filtered drinking water to Silver Bay, Beaver Bay, Two Harbors and Duluth, Minnesota. Under this plan, prepared by Russell Train's Federal Field Operations Center in Duluth, filters were to be installed on water taps at fire halls (where citizens could draw water to use at home) and in public buildings such as schools, hospitals, and restaurants. Judge Lord had ordered the U.S. Army Corps of Engineers to put the interim filtration plan into effect at its own expense. His order relied upon an amendment made to the Corps' current appropriations bill by Congressman John Blatnik, authorizing the Chief of Engineers in his discretion to provide emergency supplies of clean drinking water, on such terms as he set, to any town whose drinking water was so contaminated that it caused a substantial threat to public health. The order ignored the parts of the amendment leaving matters to the discretion of the Chief of Engineers. There had been a row within the Administration about whether to obey Judge Lord's arguably extra-legal order, which had been settled only when Assistant Attorney General for Natural Resources Wallace Johnson personally intervened with the Office of Management and Budget. He had obtained the release of the necessary funds by raising the specter of a contempt-of-court citation. The

Nuclepore filters which Gary Glass had first tested the previous winter were then installed by the Corps at eighteen fire halls, and several hundred schools, hospitals, and restaurants from Silver Bay to Duluth. The thrust of the Eighth Circuit's remarks in St. Louis was that Judge Lord's filtration order made it less urgent to shut off Reserve's discharge.

In June 1974, the Eighth Circuit announced that it was staying for another 70 days Judge Lord's order to close the Reserve plant. Under the controlling rules a Federal appellate court may not grant a motion to stay a trial court order unless the moving party shows he is likely to win a reversal of the trial court decision on the merits. In an opinion accompanying their new stay, the Eighth Circuit concluded "that Reserve appears likely to succeed . . . in its contention that its emissions into the air and water have not been proven to be a substantial health hazard." John Hills had spent weeks at trial showing that no one could determine what is a safe threshold level for exposure to asbestos, since studies had shown progressively lighter exposures to cause cancer. The Eighth Circuit now reversed this argument: if no one knew the threshold level for asbestos-induced cancers, the judges reasoned, no one could say Reserve exposed people to concentrations of amphibole fibers above the threshold.

The judges went on to say that "there is no scientific or medical certainty regarding the mechanism actually involved . . . [in] the increased rate of gastro-intestinal cancer among workers occupationally exposed to asbestos." They quoted the following exchange from Edward Fride's cross-examination of Dr. Selikoff: "Q. You don't have evidence that fibers, if they were ingested with the drinking water of Duluth would in fact, occasion a public health hazard? A. No . . . ." The judges omitted the portion of Dr. Selikoff's answer which referred to an earlier answer for amplification: "although there is no absolute proof, the kind that we ordinarily would want, there is, in my opinion, a very reasonable probability to state that this is the case." The judges acknowledged Dr. Brown's testimony that the difficulty of identifying amphibole fibers in the tissues of deceased residents by electron microscope did not show the absence of a health hazard in Duluth. But their opinion nevertheless stated that "the results of the tissue study must weigh heavily against the assessment of any demonstrated hazard to health." Having rehearsed this evidence, the judges hypothesized: "We think Doctors Brown and Selikoff share a common medical concern, but are essentially in agreement that the discharges here simply have not been proven to be a demonstrable hazard." This hypothesis was not contradicted by the letter of Dr. Brown's cautious testimony, but it did require skipping a good deal of Dr. Selikoff's testimony. The Eighth Circuit concluded: "If we are correct in our conclusion that evidence does not exist in the record on which to find Reserve's discharges to be unsafe, the district court's determination to resolve all doubts in favor of health safety represents a legislative policy judgment, not a judicial one."

Having disposed, at least tentatively, of any basis for closing the plant, the Eighth Circuit advised the parties that it was likely to affirm that Reserve was causing "the pollution of Lake Superior" in some unspecified way. The judges therefore urged the plaintiffs and defendants to try to settle the case, adding "to us there are neither heroes nor villains among the present participants in this lawsuit." As a possible step towards settlement, the Court directed that during the new 70-day stay Reserve was to submit to Judge Lord "an acceptable plan . . . for the on-land disposal of its tailings and the significant control of its air emissions." The plaintiffs would have a chance to comment on the plan and Judge Lord would then recommend whether or not to continue the stay, depending upon whether or not he found the plan to be "reasonable" and "in good faith."

The plaintiffs in the *Reserve Mining* case were at a loss what to do next. They had been successful in District Court, where Judge Lord had found that Reserve's discharges endangered public health and had ordered the plant closed, at least until Reserve's parent corporations came up with a satisfactory pollution abatement plan. But Reserve and its parent corporations had been successful in the Court of Appeals, where the Eighth Circuit had indicated it was ready to reverse Judge Lord's health findings and had ordered the plant opened. The plaintiffs could go to the U.S. Supreme Court, but there was little chance they would even be granted a hearing there. The Supreme Court heard arguments in only a small fraction of the cases appealed to it each year — those cases had to present important legal questions. In drafting their opinion, the Eighth Circuit had been careful not to make any final judgments which would raise important legal questions. They had indicated they were ready to reverse Judge Lord on the public health question, but this indication was only tentative — they might still uphold him after hearing arguments on the merits of his decision. They had ordered the Reserve plant opened, but they had also indicated that they were likely at some unspecified time to require Reserve to end its discharge into Lake Superior and control its discharges into the air.

Despite the long odds, Minnesota, Wisconsin, Michigan and the environmental groups in the *Reserve Mining* case filed an application asking the Supreme Court to vacate the Eighth Circuit's stay and close the Reserve plant. The Federal government's trial team tried to convince their superiors to join in Minnesota's application in order to demonstrate to Reserve, and to the Eighth Circuit, that the Federal government was serious about this case. John Hills argued that it was important to get the case to the Supreme Court as soon as possible, even if the Eighth Circuit had avoided making any final judgments. With each of President Nixon's appointments, the Supreme Court was becoming more conservative and more devoted to judicial restraint. Justice William O. Douglas, the one man on the Supreme Court most likely to support Judge Lord, was in his late seventies and had an electronic pacemaker implanted in his chest. Wallace Johnson, the Assistant Attorney General for Natural Resources, discussed Minnesota's application with the Solicitor General, who represents the United States whenever it appeals to the Supreme Court and traditionally protects his influence and standing before the Court by authorizing the government to appeal a case there only if he is convinced the case requires the Supreme Court's attention. At this time the Solicitor General was Robert Bork, a quiet, bearded, bespectacled legal scholar of conservative philosophy who had come to public attention during the "Saturday Night Massacre" the previous year. (Bork had assumed the title of Acting Attorney General and dutifully fired Watergate Special Prosecutor Archibald Cox after his immediate superiors, Attorney

General Richardson and Deputy Attorney General Ruckelshaus, had been dismissed for failing to do so.) Bork and Johnson agreed that it "would almost certainly be futile" to appeal the Eighth Circuit's newest stay order to the Supreme Court since it was "only a temporary ruling." They declined to join in the application.

Without the prestige of the Solicitor General's office supporting their motion, Minnesota and the remaining plaintiffs faced even longer odds. The Supreme Court rules required that they present their application to Justice Harry A. Blackmun, who was assigned to review all Eighth Circuit matters. In addition to being a strict conservative, Justice Blackmun had been a judge on the Eighth Circuit until his promotion to the Supreme Court by President Nixon. They thought it unlikely Justice Blackman would reverse his former colleagues, especially since he was also the former counsel of the Mayo Clinic, and the Eighth Circuit's opinion quoted prominently from the testimony of the Mayo Clinic's own Dr. Arnold Brown. The plaintiffs had one faint hope. Under the Supreme Court's rules they would be able to present their application to any other Supreme Court justice, if Justice Blackmun turned them down. This would leave them free to go to Justice Douglas who had, only a year before, startled the nation by ordering a halt to all United States bombing in Cambodia on a similarly-presented application. The plaintiffs did not realize this hope, however. At the beginning of July, the Clerk of the Supreme Court issued a two-sentence announcement. Justice Blackmun had referred Minnesota's application to the entire Court, rather than rule on it himself, and the Court had denied the application, over the dissent of Justice Douglas.

With the possibility of appeal gone, at least for the present, Arlene Lehto sent telegrams to the three Eighth Circuit judges on behalf of the Save Lake Superior Association, offering to send fifty-gallon drums of Duluth drinking water for them to serve their families. John Hills helped the staff of Senator Gaylord Nelson of Wisconsin draft a bill designed to reverse the Eighth Circuit's decision by statute. Once the government had shown that an industrial discharge created some risk, the bill put the burden on the polluter to prove that its discharge did not threaten public health. Liberal Congressmen and Senators from Michigan, Wisconsin and Minnesota (including Hubert Humphrey and Walter Mondale) supported the bill. Such a bill passed the Senate in the dying days of the 94th Congress, late in 1974. But a similar bill was defeated in a voice vote on the House floor by a group of conservative Congressmen, most of them from areas which had major Armco Steel plants, led by Representative Robert Jones of Alabama (who has been called John Blatnik's "Congressional lieutenant").

Following the decision of the Eighth Circuit, Reserve formally presented its Palisade Creek plan to Judge Lord, and he took evidence on it for more than three weeks. At the conclusion of these hearings, the State of Minnesota rejected the Palisade Creek plan: a tailings impoundment there would inundate a scenic wilderness area which the State Department of Natural Resources had long been considering for designation as a park. The State, joined by the Federal government at the urging of its trial team, also presented more basic objections to Judge Lord — the same objections which Reserve Vice President Kenneth Haley had presented to the Lake Superior Enforcement Conference three years earlier, when Reserve was arguing against on-land disposal near its Silver Bay plant. Such disposal was not an effective way of keeping tailings out of Lake Superior: there was always the danger of failure of one of the impounding dams, which would be constructed from tailings to a height of several hundred feet, and surface water would erode tailings from the impoundment into Lake Superior long after Reserve ceased to exist. Such an impoundment would also result in blowing dust in the nearby town of Silver Bay. This last of Reserve's three-year old objections was especially important in light of the evidence presented to Judge Lord during the trial on the devastating consequences of inhaling amphibole asbestos. Amphibole fibers in the blowing dust from a tailings impoundment near Silver Bay would compound the health risk of Reserve's continuing refusal to control air emissions from its plant, as required by Air Pollution Control Regulation No. 17. The plaintiffs pointed out that Reserve could meet these environmental objections, and lessen energy consumption at the same time, by moving its fine crushing and separating operations and disposing of its tailings farther inland, near its mine at Babbitt.

Judge Lord issued an opinion at the beginning of August, quoting Haley's testimony before the Lake Superior Enforcement Conference, and declaring that the Palisade Creek plan was not ecologically reasonable. Furthermore, since Reserve and its parent corporations had known for months the basis for the plaintiffs' rejection of the plan, Judge Lord did not consider their offer to be a good faith effort at a settlement. He recommended that the Eighth Circuit vacate its stay of his order closing the Reserve plant. Armco and Republic were still saying that the Reserve plant would never reopen, if it were closed until they agreed to dispose of their tailings near Babbitt. Looking at the economics of Reserve's operation, the plaintiffs' mining consultants thought that these threats were probably untrue. Judge Lord wrote that he had "been caught up in the corporate shell game before in this case." He chose to gamble on the probabilities that the corporations were once again not telling him the truth. Even if he was wrong and the plant did close for good, Judge Lord wrote, the closing would not do serious harm to the parent corporations: the short-term demand for steel had declined during 1974 so that Armco and Republic now had "adequate supplies of alternative ore." Nor would closing necessarily be a disaster for Reserve's workers: new taconite projects would open several thousand new construction jobs on the Mesabi Range before winter; "No one need be out of a job." He concluded: "Defendants can abate and continue to make substantial profits . . . . If Armco and Republic choose to invest their money elsewhere at the expense of their work force in Minnesota, there is little this Court can do about this decision. Such has been the history of the mining industry."

In August 1974, the Eighth Circuit held a series of hearings, not on the merits of Judge Lord's decision, but on extensions of its "temporary" stay of that decision. The judges of the Eighth Circuit personally explored the possibility of a settlement at these hearings — an unusual step for an appellate court. At the third hearing, Edward Fride announced that Reserve, Armco and Republic were willing to consider another disposal site near its Silver Bay plant, immediately south of Palisade Creek. Tailings disposal in this area, called Lax Lake, was still subject to the objections Reserve's Kenneth Haley had made at the Lake Superior Enforcement Conference. However, the Lax Lake site did not take any prospective park land. And it offered Reserve an important tactical advantage over Palisade Creek: it could blunt opposition within the government of the State of Minnesota, and within environmental groups. Lax Lake was the same area that Charles Stoddard's Taconite Study Group had suggested as a tailings disposal site six years earlier, the same area that Grant Merritt, MECCA, the Save Lake Superior Association and the Northern Environmental Council had proposed to the Lake Superior Enforcement Conference Technical Committee three years earlier. Grant Merritt and the staff of the Minnesota Pollution Control Agency were reluctant to reject Reserve's Lax Lake proposal now, but the staff of the Minnesota Department of Natural Resources remained, as it had been three years earlier, unconvinced that Reserve could not adopt the environmentally preferable alternative of disposing of its tailings near its mine at Babbitt. In light of this division, the State government reacted to the Lax Lake site equivocally, in a carefully drawn letter from Governor Anderson. The State's lawyer summarized the reaction in a single word: "maybe." The judges of the Eighth Circuit reacted favorably to Reserve's offer, despite these problems. Four months after Judge Lord had decided that Reserve's discharges into the air and water threatened public health, Reserve was still discharging. The same three Eighth Circuit judges who had begun the year by reversing Judge Lord's joinder of Armco and Republic because of their "concern that the resolution of the important 'health hazard' issue might be greatly delayed" still showed no inclination to review Judge Lord's decision on the merits. They now granted Reserve an open-ended stay of Judge Lord's order.

Once again, Minnesota prepared to apply to the Supreme Court to vacate the stay of Judge Lord's order. Now there was more pressure on the Solicitor General to lend his prestige to this application. A bureaucratic game of musical chairs helped to increase the pressure. During the summer, John Hills had left the Department of Justice to become a senior staff member of the President's Council on Environmental Quality. A governmental backwater, the Council's sole visible product was its annual report. However, Hills' job at the Council left him at least a nominal role in the *Reserve Mining* case, since the Council's chairman had the vaguely assigned duty to coordinate Federal action on Duluth's drinking water. Hills recalls, "I was conscious of the possibility of a fix after the trial was over. If I stayed at Justice I'd be under the control of the fixers and powerless to do anything. The Council was a logical 'safe home' while I was looking for a place to go into private practice." An EPA lawyer who had helped Hills at the trial took his place at the Department of Justice, and Pamela Quinn (soon to be Hills' wife) took that lawyer's place as the working-level EPA official responsible for the case. Now the Council on Environmental Quality and EPA (prompted by Hills and Quinn) both urged the Solicitor General to take action. They were supported by the remaining members of the government's trial team within the Natural Resources Division of the Department of Justice. Two lawyers for the State of Minnesota flew to Washington to call upon Assistant Attorney General Johnson, who took them upstairs to make a personal plea to Solicitor General Bork. As impressed by the splendor of Bork's office as they had once been by the squalor of John Hills' office three floors below, the Minnesota lawyers were hopeful after the meeting: Johnson had seemed to support them and Bork, while he hadn't committed himself, had at least listened. Verna Mize obtained letters from Great Lakes Congressmen to Bork, asking him to act. At the beginning of October, after three months of cajolery by the governments of the concerned States, the Congress, the Council on Environmental Quality, EPA, and the Department of Justice staff, Bork finally joined Minnesota and her fellow plaintiffs in applying to the Supreme Court to vacate the Eighth Circuit's stay or to require that the stay at least end by some definite date.

Four days later, the Supreme Court denied the plaintiffs' application. Unlike the Supreme Court's denial in July, this denial offered the plaintiffs some hope, however. For one thing, Justice Douglas had now written a scathing dissenting opinion, quoting virtually all of Judge Lord's findings, and concluding: "If equal justice is the federal standard, we should be as alert to protect the people and their right as the Court of Appeals was to protect 'maximizing profits.' If, as the Court of Appeals indicates, there is doubt, it should be resolved in favor of humanity, lest in the end our judicial system be part and parcel of a regime that makes people, the sovereign power in this Nation, the victims of the great God Progress which is behind the stay permitting this vast pollution of Lake Superior and its environs." Even more encouraging to the plaintiffs than the dissent of Justice Douglas was the Court's announcement that four justices stated explicitly they denied the application without prejudice to the plaintiffs to apply again "if the litigation has not been finally decided by the Court of Appeals by January 31, 1975." The justices of the Supreme Court rarely expressed impatience at the way a Court of Appeals was handling a pending case, so the plaintiffs hoped that the extraordinary nature of the Supreme Court's announcement might encourage the Eighth Circuit to treat their arguments on public health with a greater degree of urgency.

At last, the Eighth Circuit scheduled arguments on the merits of Reserve's appeal from Judge Lord's decision, for December 9. The court also granted the plaintiffs' motion that arguments be heard *en banc*. Normally, this would mean that all seven judges on the Eighth Circuit would consider the appeal, however the Chief Judge and Judge Gerald R. Heaney of Duluth had both disqualified themselves, leaving only two additional judges to join the original three. They were Judge Roy L. Stephenson, an Eisenhower appointee to the U.S. District Court for Iowa, elevated to the Eighth Circuit by President Nixon, and Judge Donald P. Lay, a Johnson appointee and former trial lawyer from Omaha. Judge Stephenson would probably not change the outlook of the original three-judge panel much, but former law clerks regarded Judge Lay as the brightest and least conservative member of the Eighth Circuit bench. Judge Lay, as the most senior of the five judges, would preside over their consideration of Reserve's appeal.

John Hills was no longer responsible for representing the Federal government in court, but he nevertheless suggested that the Department of Justice try yet another approach to turning the Eighth Circuit around on the *Reserve Mining* case. The June opinion of the Eighth Circuit relied heavily on selective quotations from the testimony of Dr. Arnold Brown. Hills had heard that Dr. Brown was unhappy with the way the Eighth Circuit used his testimony to deny the existence of a hazard to public health. Hills proposed that his successor at the Department of Justice take a post-trial deposition from Dr. Brown under the Federal Rules of Civil Procedure, and use his testimony to undercut the Eighth Circuit's position on the public health issue. The rules only allowed the use of post-trial depositions for a few limited purposes — and none of them allowed such use of a deposition on appeal. But if Brown's testimony on deposition were favorable, the government's lawyers would figure out some way, even if it was outside the rules, to bring that testimony to the attention of the Court of Appeals.

John Hills and the Justice Department lawyer flew to the Mayo Clinic, interviewed Dr. Brown, then went on to Minneapolis, where Dr. Brown's deposition was scheduled, just three days before the Court of Appeals argument. The deposition was taken in a large basement room of the Federal courthouse, crowded with lawyers and newspaper and television reporters. At the outset, a lawyer for Armco Steel demanded to know for what purpose the deposition was being taken. The Justice Department lawyer froze: this was the weak point of the Government's tactical ploy. Hills could no longer appear as the government's lawyer, but he quickly whispered, "Say it's for any purpose authorized by the Federal Rules of Civil Procedure." His colleague repeated his words and the crisis was passed for the moment.

Through a stream of objections by Edward Fride, Dr. Brown testified that his review of the evidence convinced him people living along the Minnesota shore of Lake Superior were being exposed to a human carcinogen — "there is no question." In assessing whether the evidence showed a hazard to public health, Dr. Brown said, the Eighth Circuit had cited his scientific conclusions (*i.e.*, that which is proven to a 95% level of certainty) without paying as much attention to his medical conclusions (*i.e.*, that which common-sense requires). But when he was asked point-blank whether Reserve's discharges created a health hazard, Dr. Brown gave a qualified and evasive response. Hills whispered to ask for a recess. While people milled about in the adjacent courthouse snackbar, Hills took Dr. Brown aside in a hallway. Hills grew red in the face. His words were insistent, bordered on abusive. He reminded Dr. Brown that the Eighth Circuit had set him up as some kind of ultimate expert, and cited him to conclude there was no health hazard. The government would not have scheduled this deposition if Dr. Brown had not personally assured Hills at the Mayo Clinic that his conclusion was contrary to that of the Eighth Circuit. Now Dr. Brown's public caution not only betrayed Hills, it betrayed Dr. Brown's medical duty by allowing Reserve to continue indefinitely subjecting people to the risk of cancer. Lawyers refer to the little sessions in which they prepare a witness to testify as "woodshedding the witness"; Dr. Brown calls the experience "being sandpapered." After several minutes of "woodshedding" or "sandpapering" Dr. Brown with a calculated display of anger, Hills returned calmly to his Justice Department colleague to say he thought it was all right to resume the deposition. A string of innocuous questions followed. Then: does the reported presence of amphibole fibers from Reserve in the air and water create a hazard to health? "Yes," Dr. Brown answered, "I consider it a hazard. My problem is in terms of trying to decide whether — just how serious a hazard it is, but in the general definition of what a hazard is, yes, I would consider it." This answer, despite its characteristic qualifications, was what Hills had been looking for: the Eighth Circuit could no longer rely on Dr. Brown to deny the existence of a health hazard.

Edward Fride opened his argument before the Eighth Circuit in St. Louis by moving that the deposition of Dr. Brown be made part of the appellate record, perhaps because the court must have known about the deposition from the newspapers, or because he thought Dr. Brown's testimony on deposition was too equivocal to harm him. No one objected to Fride's motion, so everyone agreed in effect to waive the rules. With that out of the way, Fride and his colleagues, arguing on behalf of Reserve, Armco and Republic, presented a by-now-familiar stonewall defense: "The mere fact that the government of Minnesota or the Federal government accuses and charges doesn't operate as evidence." Pollution caused by Reserve and its parent corporations "does not exist in the air or in the water . . . . There has been no pollution established in this case that is a danger to health." The companies "deny any contribution [of pollutants] to water supplies." A thorough scientific investigator found that Reserve's tailings discharge went to a "great trough" in Lake Superior, and "on no occasion did he observe that material entering surface water or leaving the confines of the great trough." "Most all of the investigators" looking at Lake Superior had found "many sources of amphibole fibers other than Reserve."

After Reserve and its parent corporations concluded their opening arguments, Judge Lay remarked, "I just can't accept some of the statements made by the appellants today that there is no pollution; I don't think that's being candid to the court." Now, as it had been before Judge Lord, the corporations' last line of defense was an almost Marxist insistence that truth must be subordinated to economics. Edward Fride warned darkly in his rebuttal argument, "I'm not sure that any of the parties to this litigation can afford a finding that there is a health hazard in Reserve's ore." It would not be "practical" for Reserve, Armco and Republic "to expend $243 million" building the Lax Lake tailings impoundment (which the Eighth Circuit saw as the solution to this controversy) "if in fact there is a demonstrable, substantial health hazard" from Reserve's tailings.

Lawyers for the United States argued that the evidence, and Dr. Brown's testimony on deposition, supported Judge Lord's findings. They asked the Eighth Circuit to affirm Judge Lord's order closing the plant and to return jurisdiction to him; he could reopen the plant if Reserve, Armco and Republic committed themselves to an acceptable abatement plan. So long as the plant stayed open, the corporations had no incentive to commit themselves to such a plan. The judges questioned Minnesota's lawyer on the status of Reserve's Lax Lake proposal. The lawyer explained that the State's Environmental Policy Act prohibited the issuance of permits for a tailings impoundment at Lax Lake, if there was a reasonable and prudent alternative less damaging to the environment. Unless Reserve came up with some convincing new evidence, he said, the company's Babbitt mine site was such an alternative and "it would be illegal to issue a permit for Lax

Lake." Judge Bright asked him if Reserve's projection of the prohibitive capital cost of relocating at Babbitt did not "seem reasonable or significant any way to you?" Minnesota's lawyer replied that it ordinarily would, but not in the context of this case. Judge Ross said, "As I interpret what you say, permits for the Lax Lake site would be issued only over your dead body, to coin a phrase." The lawyer denied this. He could only give legal advice to the State Pollution Control Agency and Department of Natural Resources; the technical people of those agencies told him that the likelihood of granting Lax Lake permits was anywhere from 5 percent to 50 percent.

After hearing four hours of arguments, the Eighth Circuit once again took the *Reserve Mining* case under advisement. A month passed, then two, then three. Well beyond the deadline suggested by four Supreme Court justices, there was still no word from the Eighth Circuit. For a third time, Minnesota applied to the Supreme Court to vacate the Eighth Circuit's stay. For a second time, the United States joined in the application. While this application was still pending before the Supreme Court, the Eighth Circuit issued a decision, rendering the application moot.

The Eighth Circuit's opinion of March 14, 1975, began with a painstaking, twenty-page analysis of the evidence in the *Reserve Mining* case, weighing the known dangers and still undefined risks of human exposure to asbestos. The analysis might well have been written by Dr. Brown or Dr. Selikoff. The judges found "that the medical and scientific conclusions here in dispute clearly lie on the frontiers of scientific knowledge." They went on to state that they were unpersuaded by the evidentiary defenses which Reserve had raised at trial — namely, that Minnesotans were not exposed to the exact type, or number, or size of asbestos fibers required to cause cancer, and that it was safe to swallow asbestos fibers. They concluded: "On this record it cannot be forecast that the rates of cancer will increase from drinking Lake Superior water or breathing Silver Bay air. The best that can be said is that the existence of this asbestos contaminant in the air and water gives rise to a reasonable medical concern for public health." Their conclusion was not as strongly worded as the conclusions of Dr. Selikoff or Judge Lord, but they declared on the basis of their conclusion that: "The existence of this risk to the public justifies an injunction decree requiring abatement of the health hazard on reasonable terms as a precautionary and preventive measure." Thus far, the Eighth Circuit's opinion read as though the bill which John Hills had helped Senator Gaylord Nelson's staff to draft had been enacted into law.

However, the Eighth Circuit, having found a "risk to public health of sufficient gravity to be legally cognizable," refused to reinstate Judge Lord's order closing the Reserve plant. As to air pollution, the court ruled that Reserve "must immediately proceed with the planning and implementation of emission controls" sufficient to reduce concentrations of amphibole fibers in the air of Silver Bay down to the normal, background levels which had been found in other American cities by investigators like William Nicholson of the Mt. Sinai School of Medicine. The Court dismissed the air pollution complaint of the United States, because no one had specifically testified that Reserve's *air* pollution created a health hazard outside Minnesota; the Federal government would have no say in defining the required air pollution control measures. The court also ruled on legal grounds that Minnesota Air Pollution Control Regulation No. 17 could not be applied to Reserve; the State of Minnesota and Reserve would have considerable room to negotiate what degree of air pollution control would be required. As to water pollution, the Eighth Circuit ruled that "Reserve shall be given a reasonable time to stop discharging its wastes into Lake Superior." This "reasonable time" included the time needed for Minnesota and Reserve to negotiate an appropriate on-land disposal site. The United States was to have no role in such negotiations beyond "offering suggestions and advice." Ten months earlier the Eighth Circuit had delayed resolution of the case, while it had Judge Lord consider the reasonableness of Reserve's on-land disposal plan. Now it warned Judge Lord: "The resolution of the controversy over an on-land disposal site does not fall within the jurisdiction of the federal courts." Almost the only area of the case in which Judge Lord might act was "ensuring that filtered water remains available in affected communities."

When Judge Lord heard the first news bulletins about the Eighth Circuit's opinion, he scheduled a hearing for the next day. At the hearing, he confessed that he had acted hastily. He had thought full jurisdiction over the case was being returned to him. Now he had a copy of the opinion in hand, and he could see that he had been mistaken. During the appellate proceedings, Judge Ross had labelled the actions of the United States "irresponsible" and "ridiculous" and had accused the State of Minnesota of "intransigence" and "lack of good faith." Judge Lord commented bitterly, "The only one that can act arbitrarily in this case is Reserve Mining. That's apparently in the record here, including the Court, the parties, the States, the Federal government and everyone else." It was now "the law of the case" that Reserve could do no wrong "and we must go on from there."

One week after the Eighth Circuit issued its decision, Wallace Johnson, the Assistant Attorney General for Natural Resources, gathered a group of staff lawyers in his cavernous, wood-panelled Justice Department office. The only outsider present was John Hills of the Council on Environmental Quality. Johnson asked the lawyers for their views on the Eighth Circuit opinion in the *Reserve Mining* case. After several minutes of discussion Johnson's deputy, Walter Kiechel, summarized the virtually unanimous view of the lawyers present: the Eighth Circuit decision was a classic *non sequitur* — it read as though there were a page missing. The decision gave the Federal government a victory on the facts and (except for its air pollution count) on the law. But it didn't grant any relief. The decision set no fixed deadlines and left Reserve free to continue discharging indefinitely while it negotiated with the badly-divided State of Minnesota over an on-land disposal site. The Federal government should not acquiesce in a decision which left it without power to stop a continuing violation of Federal law.

Assistant Attorney General Johnson did not disagree with the views of his staff. But, he said, there wasn't much he could do in light of a letter he had just received from the Justice Department's "client," EPA Administrator Russell Train. Johnson read the lawyers the letter, which hailed the Eighth Circuit opinion as "an important precedent" and requested the Department of Justice to refrain from seeking further appellate review of the opinion. Some of the lawyers laughed. Train's letter epitomized a standing joke among them. In Minneapolis bars and restaurants, John Hills occasionally recited the only literary quotation in his repertoire for the benefit of his colleagues. It was from "The Lee Shore" in *Moby Dick*: "All deep, earnest thinking is but the intrepid effort of the soul to keep the open independence of her sea . . . . Better it is to perish in that howling infinite, than be ingloriously dashed upon the lee, even if that were safety! For worm-like, then, oh! who would craven crawl to land!" The lawyers always agreed that EPA, given the chance, did "the craven crawl" with more polish than Fred Astaire did the tango. One of the most senior lawyers present remarked that if Train could write such a letter, Emperor Hirohito could, with equal plausibility, have announced on V-J Day he was stopping the war because he'd won. (A month later, another of the lawyers present was arguing in the United States District Court for Maine in favor of an injunction against the pollution of a stream by a logging company. The judge dismissed his argument impatiently. "Are you familiar with the mine dumping case on Lake Superior?" he asked the helpless lawyer. "The company there is dumping something said to cause cancer, yet that's still going on isn't it?")

John Hills was not surprised by Russell Train's letter. Pamela Quinn had called him from EPA the day before to say that Wallace Johnson had asked for a "no appeal" letter right away. Outside the Assistant Attorney General's office after the meeting, another senior lawyer, a frequent golfing partner of Johnson, explained that Johnson had been called over to the White House a few days ago, and warned about "hard-lining" against industry in environmental cases. This seemed plausible to the other lawyers. The senior lawyer had no apparent reason to lie, and the story was consistent with what they knew. When Johnson was on President Nixon's staff, he had handled a number of sensitive chores: he was a principal figure in efforts to "limit the damage" caused by charges that the White House had imposed a political settlement of antitrust actions against ITT, and to assure a friendly attitude on the part of Senator Sam Ervin's Watergate Committee. He had worked closely with Charles Colson, E. Howard Hunt and G.

Gordon Liddy. His appointment to the Department of Justice had come at a time when the White House was putting staff men in key Executive branch jobs to secure increased responsiveness to the President's wishes in the Federal bureaucracy. Now President Ford was trying to assert control over the Federal government after the chaos of Nixon's last year and project a quiet pro-business image. The scuttlebutt among Johnson's staff was that Johnson still kept in close touch with the White House staff, though no one knew for sure just how close. (When he left the Department of Justice, Johnson's 12 top staff lawyers gave him a farewell lunch. Someone remarked that there were 13 men at the table for his last meal with his subordinates. Johnson laughed, "But none of you will betray me, because I haven't put anything in writing.")

The week after the meeting in Johnson's office, Saul Friedman of the *Detroit Free Press* called Hills to talk about the *Reserve Mining* case. Hills told Friedman, he thought on a "background" basis, what had happened. A wireservice version of Friedman's subsequent story appeared in the *Washington Star* for March 25, 1975. It began, "The Justice Department, under pressure from the White House, is considering a secret recommendation to drop further appeals in the pollution case against the Reserve Mining Company on the grounds that the government has won a victory." The story went on to give a blow-by-blow account of the meeting in Johnson's office. Johnson was irate. He says, "I perceived myself as being very aggressive, given the complexities of the case. Now the implication was that I was a tool of Big Steel. It was a bum rap." He "cannot think of anything at all" that would provide any basis for the story that he had been called to the White House. Johnson called Hills' superiors at the Council on Environmental Quality to complain of Hills' breach of trust. Hills was called on the carpet. He had no more influence with the Administration's decision-makers in the *Reserve Mining* case. "The incident was painful because I was made to look disloyal to the Administration which employed me," Hills says. "But I considered myself more responsible to the public and its need to know — particularly to know that the Administration was flushing the case."

Two weeks after the Eighth Circuit decision, EPA issued a press release setting forth the contents of Russell Train's letter to Johnson and announcing "the formation of a multi-disciplinary interagency task force to monitor the clean up progress of the Reserve Mining Company." The next day, Train received a telegram of congratulations on his press release from C. William Verity, the Chairman of the Boards of Armco Steel and Reserve Mining Company. (Looking back, Verity praises the Eighth Circuit's contribution in "returning sanity to the case . . . . We have sustained all of our arguments on health. And there is no evidence of any health problem of any kind.") Train's "interagency task force" met sporadically. The sanitary engineer who Train had designated as its chairman resisted infrequent requests that the task force act, by reminding its members that "we're just supposed to protect the Administrator's ass."

Wallace Johnson formally recommended to Solicitor General Robert Bork that the United States not seek Supreme Court review of the Eighth Circuit's *Reserve Mining* opinion, but he took the unusual step of attaching a cover note that his recommendation was opposed by almost every staff lawyer responsible for the case. Hills talked quietly with the staffs of Great Lakes Congressmen, who telegraphed the Attorney General urging him to seek Supreme Court review and who wrote to EPA Administrator Train asking him to reverse his position. But there was no coordinated political pressure on the Administration for strong action against Reserve at this time, because Verna Mize, the most effective lobbyist for the cause, for once did not have enough time. She was caring for her husband, now terminally ill with cancer. At the end of the spring, Solicitor General Bork decided that the United States would not seek Supreme Court review of the *Reserve Mining* decision.

During the spring of 1975, while Federal officials in Washington were attempting to withdraw gracefully from the fight to stop Reserve Mining Company's discharge, an unusually intense storm hit Duluth and western Lake Superior. Donald Mount recalls the day during the storm when a waitress in a local restaurant brought him a glass of muddy-colored water. "I thought you filtered your water," he said. "We do," she said. He took a water sample back to the National Water Quality Laboratory for Philip Cook to analyze. Cook collected some other samples and calculated that the concentrations of amphibole fibers in Duluth's drinking water, which had been averaging 100 million per liter, were now about 2.5 billion per liter. Mount called newspaper and television reporters to his office to warn that even people who usually drank the water would be giving themselves a significant additional exposure, if they persisted in drinking tap water before the storm subsided and the fibers in the lake had a chance to settle. After the storm, Cook quietly began spot testing on the Army Corps of Engineers' water filters around town. In the restaurant where Mount had gotten the glass of muddy water, Cook found that the filter had been improperly installed so that it did not remove any amphibole fibers.

Judge Lord talked by telephone to the National Water Quality Laboratory during this period. He asked Gary Glass to survey Duluth's water filters. Glass enlisted the help of Arlene Lehto. Together they learned there was no regular program to replace filters at 11 Duluth fire halls, even though the manufacturer recommended that they be replaced every six months. There was no performance check of any kind on the remaining filters in the city. Only two-thirds of Duluth restaurants attempted to filter their drinking water; even fewer places used filtered water for ice cubes, or coffee, or in food processing. Sometimes filtered water taps were bypassed because the water came out too slowly. Many elementary schools had some drinking fountains with filtered water, some with raw water, and no distinguishing signs. Cook examined the water from one elementary school drinking fountain where he discovered the filter had failed. Not only did the sample contain amphibole fibers, it also contained a billion fiberglass fibers per liter, from the broken filter cartridge.

In the fall of 1975, Judge Lord scheduled "an unusual session of the Federal Court" to educate public officials about exposure to airborne and waterborne wastes from Reserve Mining Company. He had a United States marshall serve letters requesting the attendance of administrators of school districts along the Minnesota shore of Lake Superior, of officials of the State government and of the hearing officer who had been appointed jointly by the Minnesota Pollution Control Agency and the Department of Natural Resources to consider Reserve's application for permits to construct a tailings impoundment at Lax Lake. At the beginning of the hearing Judge Lord announced that he would "take a roll call" by having each invited official stand and identify himself. "I address all of you and admonish you that you are playing with fire . . . . Sometimes I feel like a voice in the wilderness." Moses, he said, went to the mountain top alone and received the word, and the Israelites had to trust him. "I am not comparing myself to Moses, but in this respect that it has all been here, it is all indelibly written on the record in this court. Anyone, whether it be the State in its proceedings involving just what they are going to do and how much exposure they are going to allow, who does not know — in terms of where they are dumping this stuff, and so forth — who does not know exactly what the health risk is, is derelict in their duty."

Judge Lord said he would examine some witnesses himself. Edward Fride objected to this manner of proceeding. Judge Lord told him that the record would show a continuing objection to everything he was doing, and Fride need not speak again. He told the audience, "I had nine months of hearings and two and a half years of discovery before that . . . . In every instance and under every circumstance Reserve Mining Company hid the evidence, misrepresented, delayed and frustrated the ultimate conclusions that had to be arrived at." The judge called Philip Cook to the stand. He summarized Cook's findings for the audience as "an almost total failure to give clear water in Duluth, even to those who want clear water." Judge Lord also called an engineer from the State Department of Natural Resources, who testified that heavy equipment would be operating on hundreds of acres of exposed tailings upwind of the population of Silver Bay, if Reserve built a tailings impoundment at Lax Lake. He called William Nicholson of the Mt. Sinai School of Medicine, who testified that he had observed clouds of dust blowing off other asbestos tailings impoundments and that such clouds "would constitute a health hazard to individuals exposed down wind." Nicholson also testified that Dr. Selikoff had been following 326 wives and children of amosite asbestos workers since the trial;

four of the children had already died of mesothelioma, even though "we are only now reaching the period of greatest risk." Since the trial, Nicholson had examined more samples and made new calculations which showed the air of Silver Bay already contained concentrations of amphibole fibers comparable in size and number to concentrations in the air of asbestos workers' homes. Then, Judge Lord called on Dr. Arnold Brown, who testified "based on a great deal of respect that I have for Dr. Nicholson and Dr. Selikoff and their laboratory, the faith that I have in their results . . . that there is a likelihood — I should say a real possibility — of cancers occurring in the Silver Bay area among residents of that city, secondary to the inhalation of air containing asbestiform fibers."

Judge Lord told his audience that experts from the Boston consulting firm of Arthur D. Little, Inc., now representing Reserve in the State administrative proceedings on the company's permit application for a Lax Lake tailings impoundment, had also testified for the company in his courtroom. The judge asked Nicholson to describe the role of Arthur D. Little, Inc., in resisting strict standards for occupational exposure to asbestos. Nicholson described how the firm "did not accurately report information" and "presented misinformation wrongly obtained." Judge Lord urged his audience to read about the firm and the asbestos industry in Paul Brodeur's *New Yorker* articles. He read from the bench two articles in the business press describing the role of Arthur D. Little, Inc., in resisting strict standards for occupational exposure to the cancer-causing chemical vinyl chloride: in 1974 the firm told the government that proposed standards for the vinyl chloride industry would cost 1.6 million jobs and $65 billion in lost sales and production; in 1975, six months after the standards took effect, no vinyl chloride plant had closed, four new ones had opened, and prices were below their historic highs. Judge Lord concluded that he had no faith in Arthur D. Little, Inc., and would give any evidence presented by the firm "very little credence."

As a result of Judge Lord's "educational" hearing, the first positive actions were taken to monitor water filters and to teach school children about the contamination of their drinking water.

That winter, the Army Corps of Engineers began to make free half-gallon cartons of clean drinking water available at grocery stores in all the affected communities. Also as a result of Judge Lord's hearing, Reserve Mining Company and its parent corporations moved the Eighth Circuit to remove Judge Lord from the case.

In December 1975, the Eighth Circuit held a hearing at St. Louis in a proceeding now captioned *Reserve Mining Company* v. *Honorable Miles W. Lord* . It did not take much argument from Edward Fride to demonstrate to the court that Judge Lord was now overtly hostile to the defendants in the case, that he had disregarded the Eighth Circuit's explicit direction not to interfere in the selection of an on-land disposal site, and that he had attempted to discredit the Eighth Circuit in the eyes of the public. Fifteen years earlier the Minnesota Supreme Court had censured then-Attorney General Lord *in absentia* for similar conduct. This time he was in the courtroom to argue his own case. As the judges of the Eighth Circuit sat in silence, Judge Lord began, "I appear here because of my deep concern for the welfare of the people in Lake Superior communities . . . . I have been involved in this case for nearly four years. When the case first started it was pending in an administrative agency in the State of Minnesota. Now after years of exhaustive pretrial proceedings and a nine-month trial on the merits and several appeals, the case is exactly where it was pending before, a State of Minnesota administrative agency." After a few minutes, he asked for questions. There were none. He plunged ahead. He understood, he said, "why those lawyers, their voices may quaver a little bit and they may tremble a little bit when they come before you on a very important case." He spoke of the patience with which he had considered Reserve's evidentiary defenses at trial and the reasons why he was reluctant to accept on-land tailings disposal near Silver Bay. He concluded, "The Court has said there are no heroes or no villains in this case. I sometimes feel like Reserve may have found the villain: it's the judge who exposed them for what they are."

One month later, the Eighth Circuit directed the Chief Judge of the United States District Court for Minnesota to remove Judge Lord from the case of *United States of America* v. *Reserve*

Mining Company because of his "gross bias" against the defendants and his "intentional violation of the mandate of this court." Judge Lord's removal eliminated the last official in a position of responsibility who was publicly committed to a Federal deadline for an end to the discharges of Reserve Mining Company. Despite eight years of effort, the Federal government had been unable to halt "this vast pollution of Lake Superior and its environs."

Afterword

Under the opinion of the United States Court of Appeals for the Eighth Circuit, it was within the exclusive jurisdiction of the State of Minnesota to devise some alternative to Reserve Mining Company's dumping of taconite tailings into Lake Superior. One year after the Eighth Circuit entered its opinion, the hearing officer appointed jointly by the Minnesota Pollution Control Agency and the State Department of Natural Resources recommended that Reserve's application for permits to construct a tailings impoundment at Lax Lake be denied. Like Judge Lord before him, the hearing officer cited in his opinion testimony opposing the construction of such an impoundment, given by Reserve at the Lake Superior Enforcement Conference in 1971. He found that "the best evidence on fiber content per unit of dust emanating from a tailings disposal area" was the testimony of Philip Cook, who was continuing to examine samples of Reserve's tailings and samples taken from the air outside the public schools of Silver Bay. The hearing officer concluded that, even if Reserve eventually controlled dust emissions from its plant, blowing dust from a Lax Lake impoundment would actually *increase* the present alarming levels of amphibole fibers in the air of Silver Bay. He acknowledged testimony by officials of Reserve, Armco and Republic that denial of the Lax Lake permit applications "would likely lead to shutdown." However, he noted dryly that Reserve's projected cost (now raised to $749 million) for moving its fine crushing and separating operations inland, near its mine at Babbitt, was "contrary to recent experience in the expansion of other taconite facilities." It was, he concluded,

191

"impossible to determine in advance" if denial of the permit applications would cause Reserve to cease operations. The citizen board of the Pollution Control Agency and the Commissioner of the Department of Natural Resources accepted the recommendations of the hearing officer and denied Reserve's application for permits to construct a tailings impoundment at Lax Lake.

Reserve appealed the decision of the Minnesota Pollution Control Agency and the Department of Natural Resources to a State District Court panel of three judges, including C. Luther Eckman, who had approved Reserve's deep pipe plan six years earlier. The three State judges ordered the agencies to grant Reserve's application. They "suggested" that Judge Lord's "educational hearing" of November 1975 had improperly influenced the hearing officer and the agencies. They found no substantial evidence to support the hearing officer's reliance on the somber warnings of Philip Cook about the amphibole fiber levels which a Lax Lake tailings impoundment would produce in the air of Silver Bay. They gave equal weight to far lower projections made for Reserve by Arthur D. Little, Inc. Finally, the judges stated, it was "unreasonable" to disregard the corporations' threat that they would close if their Lax Lake permit applications were denied. The Minnesota Supreme Court upheld the decision of the three judges. (The court noted that Chief Justice Robert Sheran, Reserve's former trial lawyer, took no part in the decision of the case.) The State agencies then issued the permits.

On March 16, 1980, Reserve Mining Company completed construction of a tailings impoundment at Lax Lake. On that date Reserve ceased discharging taconite tailings into Lake Superior.

In the meantime, the City of Duluth constructed a filtration plant which removed most of Reserve's tailings from the intake of its water supply, fulfilling the prediction made by its health officer 30 years earlier. Reserve, Armco and Republic were ordered to pay all the interim costs of filtration by Edward D. Devitt, the Chief Judge of the United States District Court for Minnesota, an Eisenhower appointee, who replaced Judge Lord on the *Reserve Mining* case. The corporations argued that they were not solely responsible for the contamination of drinking water along the Minnesota shore of Lake Superior, but he concluded that Judge Lord's findings were based on "overwhelming evidence" and that "Reserve is responsible for essentially all of the amphibole asbestos fibers found in the public drinking water of the relevant communities." He curtly dismissed as "fatuous" the corporations' argument that they were being assessed damages for injuries which were "only speculative." He stated, "It is not required by law, or by common sense, that illness and death are conditions precedent to taking preventive measures against such a health hazard."

Judge Devitt also upheld Judge Lord rigorously in the other areas which remained within his jurisdiction under the Eighth Circuit's opinion. He fined Reserve, Armco and Republic $837,000 for violating the terms of Reserve's original 1947 permit from the State of Minnesota. He also held that Reserve had "thwarted all settlement efforts and made final resolution of the issues presented more difficult" by contending in bad faith that the deep pipe was the only feasible alternative method of disposal. This contention had been made possible, he said, by Reserve's continuing misconduct — beginning when the company "did not truthfully and fully respond to plaintiffs' interrogatories." He dismissed Reserve's defense of its conduct as "frivolous" and "a belated rationalization." He fined Reserve $200,000 for its violations of court rules and orders. The Eighth Circuit affirmed each of Judge Devitt's rulings on appeal.

The health consequences to Duluth citizens of drinking water containing Reserve's tailings for more than 20 years are the subject of continuing scientific research. Epidemiological studies of the general population are necessarily somewhat imprecise. But continuing epidemiological studies conducted by the Minnesota Department of Health do strongly suggest that people who take their drinking water from western Lake Superior have not experienced the dramatic increases in cancer rates which are associated with the occupational inhalation of asbestos dust.

The results of other scientific studies are more sobering, however. A study completed by Dr. Arnold Brown contradicts the testimony of Dr. Paul Gross for Reserve; his study includes electron microscope photographs of amphibole asbestos fibers caught in the act of penetrating the gastrointestinal tract wall of laboratory mice. Philip Cook has also published in *Science* a study demonstrating that amphibole fibers swallowed in Duluth drinking water spread throughout the human system. Cook used an electron microscope to examine concentrated urine samples from volunteers drinking Duluth water; since the urinary tract functions to carry away impurities removed from the blood by the kidneys, he reasoned that the presence of amphibole fibers in urine would demonstrate that such fibers were circulating in the blood stream. His study shows a close correlation between the amount of amphibole fibers swallowed in drinking water and the amount in the urine. Cook says, "The tissue study proposed by Dr. Selikoff and the court didn't find statistically significant numbers of amphibole fibers, but, in retrospect, the study used inappropriate electron microscope techniques. My later work suggests that the body retains something like one fiber out of every 1,000 swallowed in Duluth drinking water. If this is correct, then there should have been only *one* amphibole fiber in all of the tiny amount of tissue that was examined in the court study. Of course, we still haven't proved just how many amphibole fibers must be retained in the tissue before there is an increased incidence of cancer."

Donald Mount says that Cook's study is "one of the most conclusive pieces of evidence to date that asbestos fibers are a hazard to your health whether they're inhaled or ingested." But, Mount warns, "there may never be a point at which science says 'It has been proven beyond doubt that taconite tailings in drinking water cause cancer.' Look at the years of scientific work on cigarette smoking and cancer. What's more probable is a slow accumulation of pieces of evidence like Dr. Brown's study and Phil's study — nails in the coffin — until only the most irrational people believe the opposite."

INDEX